SNOWBOARDING

SKILLS

TRAINING

TECHNIQUES

CROWOOD SPORTS GUIDES

SNOWBOARDING

SKILLS

TRAINING

TECHNIQUES

Dan Wakeham with Sophie Everard

THE CROWOOD PRESS

First published in 2013 by
The Crowood Press Ltd
Ramsbury, Marlborough
Wiltshire SN8 2HR

www.crowood.com

© The Crowood Press 2013

British Library Cataloguing-in-Publication Data
A catalogue record for this book is available from the British Library.

ISBN 978 1 84797 520 1

All photographs are by Penny Cross, except where indicated otherwise.

Typeset by Jean Cussons Typesetting, Diss, Norfolk
Printed and bound in India by Replika Press Pvt Ltd

CONTENTS

PREFACE

Snowboarding is an exciting sport that charges its participants with adrenalin. Not only does it keep you extremely fit and active through the winter months, it takes you into the world of a competitive sport that is very lifestyle driven and exhilarating. Compared to skiing, snowboarding is still considered to be a relatively new sport, having been included in just four Winter Olympic Games. However, in that short space of time the practice, popularity and coverage of snowboarding has soared, and the slopes of the world have seen a major change from being nearly 100 per cent dominated by skiers, to the split being practically 50:50 between snowboarders and skiers.

In the early days of snowboarding, mainstream media was quick to paint a caricature of the snowboarder as a wayward and dangerous adolescent who was a menace to the mountain slopes. But snowboarding has now enjoyed a complete image turnaround and has developed into an extremely popular and profitable industry. Global snowboard competitions, such as the halfpipe in the Winter Olympics, are given nearly full television coverage and receive terrific viewing figures, if not nearly the lion's share, as in the case of the recent Vancouver 2010 Winter Olympics. The professional snowboarder now enjoys a lucrative and rewarding career, bolstered by brand sponsorship and celebrity exposure, their earnings pushing them to the upper echelons of athlete income.

Shaun White at the Burton European Open 2009, Laax, Swizterland. (© Nick Atkins)

This book offers an in-depth understanding of the sport, charting its history from its infancy to the current day, with a detailed account of its rapid development, and its acceptance into the world of competitive sport. An insight into the equipment needed, exactly how to set up a snowboard, and a run-down of the various disciplines, from the Olympic (including the halfpipe, snowboard cross and the parallel slalom) to the non-Olympic (slopestyle, big air and freeride), are covered in extensive detail.

The first experience of the snow park may be somewhat daunting and intimidating for any snowboarder, but the park will be fully described, as will its accepted 'rules', which are in place to avoid accidents and crashes. How to tackle jumps – or 'kickers', as they are commonly referred to – for the first time, and of course how to land from them, will be covered, as will the rather bewildering terminology commonly used in snowboarding, which to an outsider would seem like a foreign language.

Each section is carefully illustrated, and embellished with tips and techniques, sequence photography and diagrams. The correct techniques across each discipline, both Olympic and non-Olympic, are carefully described in order to give a concise understanding of these very different styles of snowboarding. Finally, tips for competition preparation, both for yourself and for your equipment, are addressed, and advice given on how you would make a career out of this dynamic sport.

This book is intended to be as accessible to newcomers to the sport as to more experienced snowboarders.

PART I

AN INTRODUCTION TO SNOWBOARDING

CHAPTER I

SNOWBOARDING THROUGH THE YEARS

Skateboarding and surfing are closely linked to snowboarding, and the very roots of snowboarding can in fact be traced to these sports. Boardsports have long co-existed and their origins are firmly linked: the simple fact is that during the 1950s, American skateboarding and surfing enthusiasts desired to transfer these sports on to the snow, and the early pioneers of snowboarding used self-made boards to achieve this.

This revolutionary approach to 'mountain surfing' evolved quickly, and the early prototypes of what would now be recognized as a modern snowboard were built and patented during the 1960s by Michigan engineer Sherman Poppen, who christened his invention a 'snurfer', or 'ski

Jake Burton with one of his own snowboards. (Courtesy The Burton Corporation)

board'. Poppen's creation was essentially a pair of skis strapped together, with a rope attached to the nose of the board to be held for extra control. These somewhat rickety contraptions were used by a minority, and snowboarding was not permitted in all mainstream ski resorts. Nevertheless, despite a less-than-positive reception to these innovative 'ski boards', snowboarding was quick to develop an underground following, with participants avoiding the busy slopes dominated by skiers (where they were not accepted in any case), seeking the back country tracks of the mountain to experiment.

By the mid-1970s the snurfer was evolving and maturing: a new breed of board called the 'winterstick' was developed by college graduate Dimitrije Milovich, whose subsequent creation of the snowboard was more heavily influenced by surfboards. By this time Jake Burton, one of the most infamous names in the history of snowboarding, and an individual who still dominates the snowboard industry to this day with his innovative company 'Burton Snowboards', was developing his own version of the snurfer, which had fascinated him as a youth.

Vermont-based Burton's one major addition to the classic snowboard shape was the addition of snowboard 'bindings', the fastenings attached to the board which hold the rider in, now an essential part of a snowboard. Burton entered the first ever World Snurfing Championship with his own version of a snowboard in 1979, and it is at this moment that snowboarding was established as a legitimate competitive sport.

Not dissimilar to Burton's efforts were those of Tom Sims. The history of snowboarding cannot be covered without mentioning Sims, for it was Sims who

Jake Burton in the early years. (Courtesy The Burton Corporation)

really brought snowboarding to the forefront of winter sports, signing ground-breaking deals with mainstream companies and bringing heavier skateboard influences to his designs. Sims was also a pioneer in competitive snowboarding: in 1983 he helped to organize the world's first halfpipe snowboard competition in California.

Different styles of snowboarding were also quick to become established. Some snowboarders hiked into the backcountry to pick challenging mountain descents, and this became known as 'freeriding'. For others it was a race from top to bottom, and alpine or snowboard cross was born. Riders more heavily influenced by skateboarding would try to emulate

skateboard tricks, and 'get air' (use boost-off jumps and enjoy a few seconds free-fall before coming to land), the prelude to freestyle snowboarding. With freestyle rapidly developing during the 1980s, greatly assisted by both Sim's and Burton's new snowboard models, largely evolving from the early snurfer, snowboard tricks were christened with the very names of the skateboard tricks that inspired them. A 'chicken salad' or 'stale fish grab' are just two of the unique names used for some of the most famous skateboard and snowboard tricks.

Terje Haakonsen is often credited as being the 'godfather' of modern freestyle snowboarding, and the Norwegian pioneer played a huge role in shaping freestyle snowboarding into the sport that we recognize today. Terje's groundbreaking contributions to freestyle snowboarding include the legendary 'Haakon flip', and his extraordinary style and amplitude (height achieved whilst boosting on a snowboard) are widely credited as playing a major role in the progression of snowboarding.

In more recent times, Shaun White, perhaps the most prominent and indeed at least the most commercially successful of all snowboaders, was credited with boosting the progression of freestyle snowboarding to even higher and more extraordinary levels. In particular was his astonishing halfpipe trick the 'Tomahawk', a 'double mctwist 1260' (in simpler terms, this is three full rotations and two full flips, whilst boosting out the pipe), which was publicly revealed to great accolade during the Vancouver 2010 Winter Olympics. Considering that snowboarding only first appeared during the 1998 Winter Olympics in Nagano, Japan, this is a staggering progression, and indeed, snowboarding is characterized by the fast pace of its development.

Historically, snowboarding has of course drawn inspiration from surfing and skateboarding, although in recent years it would appear that skateboarders, surfers and even skiers are looking towards snowboarding for ideas. Skiers have turned to freestyle and draw their inspiration from snowboard tricks and

Terje Haakonsen in Mammoth doing a backside air on a hip. (Courtesy Adam Moran, The Burton Corporation)

style, and freestyle skiing now draws as big a crowd as classic ski events such as the giant slalom. Surfers are now experimenting with the inverts most commonly attributed to freestyle snowboarding, and are adopting the names from snowboarding.

Snowboarding has seen a rapid development. It has matured from a furtive fad which alarmed skiers and gave the snowboarder a less-than-attractive image as a dangerous, out-of-control mountain menace, to a multi-million-pound industry represented by clean-cut, committed athletes who enjoy an affluent profession and all the benefits that can be reaped from a successful sporting career.

Snowboarding and snowboarders across the world share different backgrounds and experiences of snowboarding – for example in the UK, many people's experience of snowboarding is gained via trips to the dry ski slope or indoor snow dome, which of course differs greatly to a snowboarder hailing from a mountain resort. Nevertheless, the dry ski slopes and indoor snow domes of the UK are responsible for producing a large amount of our country's best talent, athletes who enjoy as much success as those snowboarders who had the advantage of an upbringing where mountain riding was easily accessible.

CHAPTER 2

THE SNOWBOARD DISCIPLINES

Once snowboarding was admitted to the Nagano Winter Olympics in 1998 and accepted as a legitimate sport, it was decided that two snowboard disciplines would be used: the halfpipe (freestyle snowboarding) and the giant slalom (traditional ski snowboarding).

The introduction of snowboarding to the Olympics caused a controversial split amongst snowboarders. Some felt that it was the natural progression of the sport, others felt that by allowing a ski federation (the FIS, or *Fédération Internationale du Ski*) to take charge of the sport's direction, snowboarding would lose its identity and uniqueness. As we move forward to the present and consider the last Winter Olympic Games in Vancouver,

A competition-built halfpipe.

Canada, snowboarding was one of the most highly viewed televized events. Some attribute this to the 'wow' factor of two-time Olympic gold medallist Shaun White's trick roster, including the already mentioned 'Tomahawk' that was exhibited by White to ecstatic crowds.

According to NBC, snowboarder Shaun White has 'single-handedly transformed snowboarding into a mainstream event'. Shaun, also known for his flame-coloured red hair and aptly nicknamed the 'Flying Tomato' by his legions of fans, is representative of the young and impressive generation that brand managers cherish. As a highly marketable athlete, Shaun White boasts a cabinet of

Ben Kilner at the Burton European Open 2012 in Laax, Switzerland, doing a frontside air. (© Nick Atkins)

impressive gold medals from both the Olympic Games and the 'X Games', the most celebrated annual competition for extreme sports, and he is the highest paid non-salaried athlete in the Winter Games.

The Olympic Disciplines

The Halfpipe

A halfpipe can be described as a pipe or tube cut in half and laid on the floor, and then its replica built out of icy snow. The walls of the pipe stand at a staggering 22ft high, and snowboarders ride in and out of it, boosting out of the lip of the pipe into the sky while performing tricks, spins, flips and grabs. They are judged on their amplitude (height out of the pipe), the technical difficulty of their performance, and the overall impression. The idea is to make it look as easy and relaxed as possible, which is awarded greater points.

Zoe Gillings at the British snowboarding championships 2010 pumping for speed and at the start gate. (Courtesy @zoegillings)

Kevin Pearce performs a frontside air at the Burton European Open 2009, at Laax. (© Nick Atkins)

Snowboard Cross

Largely considered to be one of the best Olympic spectator sports in snowboarding, snowboard cross is a high speed and often high drama discipline. Four riders at a time compete to negotiate a thrilling course of icy corners, sudden bumps and jumps, in a fast-paced race to the finish line. Accidents in snowboard cross are common, owing to the speed and the number of riders.

Slopestyle

Slopestyle is fast developing into one of the most popular and well reported competitive events in snowboarding. This is reflected in the recent decision taken by the International Olympic Committee (the IOC) to include men and women's slopestyle snowboarding in the upcoming Sochi 2014 Winter Olympics in Russia. A slopestyle course includes a mixture of different freestyle disciplines where the challenge is to find

Terje Haakonsen at Pemberton, British Columbia. (Courtesy Adam Moran, The Burton Corporation)

the best overall or most consistent rider. It includes a mixture of jumps, rails and challenging features. The idea is to include various freestyle disciplines where snowboarders have to prove their overall skill on a run that resembles a snow park. Slopestyle as a discipline has more competitors than you would find at any other event.

Parallel Slalom

Slalom racers are much like the ski racers of snowboarding. They wear lycra outfits and ride boards that are long, thin and stiff. Their boots are much like ski boots and their bindings point forwards with steep angles. Slalom snowboarding seems to be a dying breed, and snowboard racing equipment is not easy to come by; the boards often have to be made to order.

Non-Olympic Disciplines

Big Air

Snowboarders boost off a large, straight-faced wedge of snow, and are thrown into the air towards a steep landing. The art is to judge the correct speed so as not to miss the perfect or 'sweet spot' landing zone. The snowboarders perform tricks much as they would in the half pipe, and once again they are judged on their style and control, and the technical difficulty of their routine.

Freeriding

Riding inaccessible mountains and terrain is an intrinsic part of freeriding. Many snowboarders use helicopters to reach these remote areas. Competitions are held where the contestants are dropped off on top of the mountain. They are then judged on their descent. Points are added for the snowboarder who chooses the most creative 'line' — the carefully considered descent and path down the mountain.

CHAPTER 3

CONSTRUCTION OF A SNOWBOARD

As you read through this book you will start to recognize recurring terminology that is specific to snowboarding. Some words will be familiar if you have an understanding of skiing, surfing or skateboarding. Board and ski sports are considered to be cross-over sports, so many of the techniques, movements and balance skills are similar and relevant. For example, if you ski, you will already have an understanding of 'edge control' – although it is important not to assume that because you are already proficient at one of these cross-over sports, you will naturally be good at the other.

Snowboards are composed of a number of different materials, although designs from different manufacturers do vary. Nevertheless most snowboards on

Top sheet of a Head snowboard.

the market use the same construction and materials, so the following breakdown of a snowboard is relevant to most designs.

The Core

The centre or core of the snowboard is generally made of wood. This is rather like the backbone of the board. The wood is a mix of laminated wood strips, mostly placed vertically. The choice of wood construction governs how the snowboard will essentially 'work', how it moves, flexes and rides. The wood is laminated in different directions to offer different flex patterns, stiffness or aggressiveness. Some brands offer 'honeycomb' (an extremely light platform) or aluminium for their top end boards; this dramatically reduces the weight of the snowboard but can compromise the strength.

Fibreglass

The next layer of the board is usually made of fibreglass and is bonded to the core. Again, the directions of the fibres are positioned to add extra structure, strength and performance. Steel inserts are fastened into the core of the snowboard, and screw-holes protrude

through the fibreglass so that the bindings fasten securely.

Top Sheet

Materials that make up the top sheet of the snowboard include nylon, polyester or plastic. The top sheet protects the snowboard from scratches and also displays the graphics.

Base

The material used for the base is a low-friction plastic called 'polyethylene', often referred to as 'p-tex'. There are two variations of base: one is sintered, made from p-tex powder, which is pressurized and then cut into shape. Sintered bases absorb wax more efficiently, but are more expensive and harder to repair. Extruded bases are harder wearing and are often used on less expensive boards. The p-tex is heated and forced through a mould to create the appropriate shape. Extruded bases need little wax and are low maintenance, so are a good choice for the beginner snowboarder. Graphite bases are used on high-end race boards: these are sintered bases that contain a percentage of graphite to reduce friction.

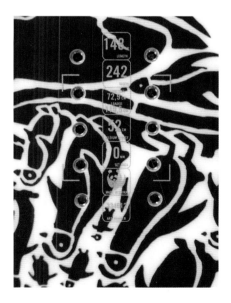

Screw-holes protrude through the fibreglass on top of a snowboard so that the bindings fasten securely.

Base of a Head snowboard.

Some brands leave the finished snowboard with a base structure. Like treads on a tyre, snowboard bases need structure to reduce drag. The board needs to ride on a film of water produced from the friction of its base cutting through the snow. Some board factories finish their bases with a golf-ball effect, which is useful on wet snow. Pockets of air between the base and the snow mean that water is repelled or displaced from the base, reducing the braking effect (like a glass sliding on a table). On cold, dry snow, the base should be as smooth as possible so the points of friction are minimized.

Edges

The snowboard is belted along the base side with a steel edge, which is set into the fibreglass. The edges offer the snowboard grip on hard or icy snow, and are used to carve and turn, and, as the snowboard 'breaks', to stop. A layer of rubber is used between the edges and fibreglass to absorb vibration.

Edges of a snowboard.

CHAPTER 4

CHOOSING YOUR SNOWBOARD AND BASIC EQUIPMENT

Snowboards come in all shapes and sizes, so how do you know which is the best for you? It is not simply a question of which snowboard is most visually attractive.

Most companies make boards in variations of three key styles: camber, rocker and flat base.

Camber: This is the traditional style. As you lay the board on the floor, both the tip and the tail will be touching the floor, but the centre will be raised. This is the most aggressive type of snowboard, and the style is used for boards that are made for maximum control at speed.

Rocker: This is the opposite of a camber snowboard in that the tip and tail are raised while the centre sits on the ground. The style is used for freestyle boards, but is also great for beginner boards, the benefit being that the board can pivot with greater ease through turns, therefore reducing the chance of the edges catching. The disadvantage is that by lifting the nose and tail from the snow, the edge length also loses contact, which reduces the board's grip on icy or hard snow; it would also lose stability at high speeds.

Flat base: A compromise between the camber and the rocker snowboard. The ride on a flat-base snowboard isn't as lcose as you would expect from a rocker board, and not as aggressive as a camber board. It is a good option for a beginner, or the freestyle rider who would like to progress their riding and attempt bigger kickers or the halfpipe.

The next option would be to choose between a twin-tip or directional

ABOVE: Subvert Boardstore sell a variety of snowboards.

RIGHT: Dom Harington, frontside air out of a halfpipe. (© Nick Atkins)

snowboard. The best way to explain this would be that a twin-tip board resembles a skateboard, in that it works equally well in any direction, whereas a directional board works best in a forward direction.

Snowboards for the Beginner

For a beginner, choosing a snowboard is easy. The board should be quite basic with a medium to short flex. Choosing the length is not just about your height,

but also how much you weigh. Some brands offer a recommended size chart of the snowboard you should be using. Generally, a safe option is to hold the board up in front of you: a board that is the correct size will stand taller than the base of your neck, but no higher than your nose. A longer snowboard will offer stability, but it may be harder to negotiate turns with it. A shorter board will feel 'looser' and is therefore a better board for freestyle, but it will feel unstable at speed.

Choosing the snowboard width depends on the size of your feet. Lay the snowboard on the carpet and stand on it: if your toes and heels hang over the edges, then the board is too narrow; if they are too far from the edges, then the board is too wide. In fact choosing a

Subvert Boardstore offer honest, friendly and knowledgeable advice. They have two stores, one in Manchester – Chill Factore – and the other in Castleford – Xscape – as well as an online shop.

snowboard is a relatively straightforward process, and if the board is a little too long/short/wide/narrow, it is not a huge problem – just make sure it is not drastically wrong for you!

A good snowboard shop employee should be able to help you choose a board that is right for you, and a good snowboard shop should therefore be your first option when buying a board. They will have a wealth of knowledge as to the snowboards and brands that they are selling, and will offer useful advice, and help you select a snowboard that is the correct style and size for you.

Snowboards for the More Advanced

As riders progress with their snowboarding, they will naturally gravitate towards the disciplines that they enjoy the most. For example, some people with a background in skateboarding may like to replicate their skateboard tricks on the snow, so they would be interested in riding 'rails' – the long metallic rails in snow parks – 'buttering', where they pivot on the nose or tail of the snowboard to spin round, so-called because the manoeuvre resembles spreading butter on to bread with a knife, or 'jibbing', meaning to snowboard on rails, spin on the flat, and tap obstacles with the snowboard.

Subvert's shop assistant Sarah Fish offers advice to customer Matt Roddis.

Aimee Fuller jibbing.

A snowboard should be higher than the base of your neck but no higher than your nose when held upright in front of you.

The most suitable board for this freestyle discipline would be almost squashed in shape, shorter in length (chest height) in order to reduce spin weight, but also wider, to maximize the surface area for float in the snow. The 'jibber' snowboarder may choose a rocker or a flat-base board.

The surfing-inspired snowboarder would be interested in carving big turns and 'slashing' as much powder snow as possible, and would be looking for snow or banks on which to perform surf-style 'slashes'. The board used for this would be slightly longer (reaching to between the nose and eyebrows), and could be camber, flat or rocker; it would most likely be directional or with a setback stance (where your binding is set back on the board to allow a longer nose for floating in powder snow). The benefit of the extra length is that it allows better 'float' – it does not sink into deep powder snow and can navigate the surface quickly.

The aggressive freestyle snowboarder who is looking to tackle large jumps will need a board that handles well at high speed, as too would an aggressive snowboard racer, boarder crosser or pipe rider. The snowboard used in this circumstance would be camber, and have a stiffer flex. The aggressive freestyle rider would require a chin-length, twin-tip board for riding in both directions.

The racer would choose a nose-length board that is directional and very stiff for maximum grip and stability at high speed. Furthermore the board would be narrower to allow quicker edge-to-edge transitions.

Side Cut

Look down the profile of a snowboard and you will notice that the waist of the board is thinner than at the nose and tail.

This curve in the edge is called the 'side cut', and there are various radiuses for different riding styles. Thus a freestyle board may have a smaller or tighter radius to help it turn more quickly at low speeds, whereas a race board would have a long,

slow radius for high-speed turns. A freeride board may have a slow radius that tightens at the tail, because most of the riding is done at the back of the snowboard, and the nose is long in order to achieve float in deeper snow.

Dan Wakeham skims over water.

Jamie Nicholls flying from a kicker.
(© Nick Atkins)

The most common binding seen in snowboard shops will be a basic freestyle binding. For many snowboarders, this style is suitable for most levels of snowboarding experience.

To fit a binding, stand in it with a snowboard boot on: the binding should fit your boot well, and your toes should not hang too far over the front of the foot bed. Ratchet up the bindings so they are comfortably tight, and stand up as if you were stood on your snowboard; be aware of any pressure points that could become uncomfortable after a full day's snowboarding. Boots also vary, of course, so be sure that your boot integrates well with the binding.

Boots

You should be picking up a common theme by now, namely that the stiffer the kit, the more aggressive it is – and it is no different with snowboard boots. Selecting

Dan Wakeham adjusts his bindings.

Bindings

Like snowboards, bindings come in different styles. Some are extremely adjustable, others are very basic; some brands offer bindings with alternative entry systems, aimed at saving time and effort. As with stiffer snowboards, stiffer bindings are indicative of a more aggressive performance, although by adding performance you may sacrifice comfort.

The high back is adjustable and can be leaned forwards to hold a steeper angle: this is called 'forward lean'. The steeper the angle, the more responsive the binding becomes, and the more quickly your board will react to small movements, meaning that less effort will be needed to put the board into a carve turn. This is relevant if you are an experienced snowboarder or racer, but your riding will need more attention because a lack of concentration could result in an edge catch and a fall.

A selection of snowboard bindings on display in Subvert Boardstore.

a boot that fits is just the same as choosing a shoe that fits you comfortably. Note that snowboard boots are designed to keep your feet warm and to be worn with snowboard socks, so it is best to buy the correct size and not allow an extra size for thicker socks.

It is essential that the snowboard boot is comfortable, because ill-fitting boots can be extremely painful. You should be able to move your toes, but not have room to move your foot from side to side. Your heel should not lift significantly when you walk. Remember, if they are new boots, they will 'break in' and soften with use. If the liner is heat mouldable, as it is in many snowboard boots, it will feel as if the boot is pressing into the top and bottom of your feet. This is normal, but only to begin with, and it will change to match the profile of your foot in less than an hour of wear.

Union Contact Pro Binding: some chief components include the triple zone-injected EVA bushings for superlative dampening, contact pro Dupont™ Sytel® ST highbacks for maintaining flexibility and stability in all conditions, and CNC-machined heelcups that drastically reduce the overall weight. (© Subvert Boardstore)

It is essential that boots fit comfortably when tied up.

Thirty-Two Boot TM2 Scott Stevens: solid and supportive, the advanced shell construction creates high-performing, smooth-flexing boots that are easier to lace and more durable. (© Subvert Boardstore)

Union Superpro Binding-Black. The 2013 Union Superpro snowboard binding is a super-tech lightweight, all-mountain freestyle destroyer, delivering a ton of custom-made parts. Strong, light hardware completes this sensational all-mountain freestyle binding. (© Subvert Boardstore)

CHAPTER 5

OTHER EQUIPMENT NEEDED

Although it is possible to rent snowboard equipment when you visit slopes, it is of course always preferable to have your own kit.

Basic Equipment

Trousers and Jackets

Trousers and jackets will not seem important until you venture out on the mountain on a day with testing conditions. Weather conditions can change very quickly, so it is essential to be prepared. For example, good quality equipment is designed to cope with diverse weather, from warm mornings to cold afternoons when sudden storms roll in, which is typical on the mountains. If your body is still damp from perspiring, then you will immediately feel extremely cold.

Good base layering is also vital. Technical t-shirts draw the sweat and moisture away from the skin so that the jacket can 'breathe' efficiently. The 'breathability' of snowboard outerwear and layers has developed rapidly as a crucial part of snowboard kit. A snowboard jacket needs to be waterproof to keep any wet snow from getting to the body, so accordingly there are ratings for its level of waterproofing. The jacket will have an additional rating for how well it will allow moisture to leave, hence aptly named 'breathability'. When buying a jacket, you will notice on the label classifications such as '8000 waterproof' and '8000 breathable': the higher the numbers, the better quality will be the fabric used in the jacket. Many brands use 'Gore-Tex' fabrics for their pants and jackets, and 'Gore-Tex' is widely regarded as the leader in technical fabric.

ABOVE: Aimee Fuller sits ready with all her snowboarding kit.

LEFT: Snowboard kit can be bought from any good snowboard store. (© Subvert Boardstore)

Animal snowboard jacket.

Goggles

Goggles are a vital part of the snowboard kit. Sunglasses do not offer adequate

protection, and are likely to be lost when jumping or snowboarding at faster speeds, so goggles are the wisest option. Goggles protect the eyes from damaging UV-light, the most important of its functions. The majority of goggles are sold with interchangeable lenses, often one chrome (silver) and the other orange: chrome lenses are for bright sunlight, offering maximum protection against strong sun, and orange lenses are for 'low light', or cloudy days. Note that even though it may not be sunny, the sun's rays can still have a damaging effect. The expression 'flat light' is a term commonly used when the light is extremely low and visibility almost at zero.

It is also possible to buy flat-light lenses, which are designed to pick out definition in low light conditions – although these are expensive. During periods of flat light it is also sensible to head towards an area with trees, as their shadows will increase your awareness of your surroundings and the ground in front of you.

Helmet

It is of course highly recommended that

Red Asylum helmet: Airvanced Ventilation™, durable-injected ABS shell, long-haired fleece on liner and ear pads, REDphones™ audio accessory compatible. (© Subvert Boardstore)

you wear a helmet whilst snowboarding. Snowboarding can be a dangerous, high impact sport, and head injuries are a common occurrence. Whatever the speed or force of an impact, serious accidents can happen regardless, and a helmet offers the best protection for your head against major injury.

Body Armour

Body armour is not an essential part of the snowboard kit, however it is recommended because it does offer ample protection against a heavy fall. Many snowboarders wear 'impact shorts', which closely resemble cycling shorts with built-in pads to protect the areas often on the receiving end of a fall, most notably the coccyx in snowboarding. Whilst learning to snowboard, you will spend time learning to fall, so impact shorts are a sensible option.

Other common protection includes the back protector, which resembles a strong, supportive shell for the spine and back. Back protectors are still discrete when worn underneath a snowboard jacket, and work by displacing the pressure points in the event of you falling on your back, thereby preventing injury.

Oakley Airbrake Snow Goggle with interchangeable lenses suitable for different weather conditions.

Red total impact shorts.

The ProTec IPS underglove wrist guards keep your wrists stable to help prevent injury.

The Protec back pad protector offers spine protection for those who want peace of mind in the event of a hard slam. Stretch gore shoulder straps and waistband keep the back pad in place for all-day comfort, while the anatomical injection-moulded and hinged spine caps and EVA foam provide the protection. (© Subvert Boardstore)

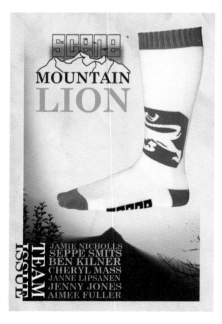

Scene socks designed by snowboarders for snowboarders.

Socks

Snowboard socks are an important part of the snowboard kit. Padded in some areas and thinner in others, snowboard socks offer comfort in your snowboard boots. The thinner areas are placed in spots on the foot where the material is likely to ruck up together, thus reducing the chances of your sock rubbing uncomfortably against your foot and your snowboard boot.

Gloves

It is sensible and advisable to own a few pairs of gloves, to be used in

Grenade gloves.

different conditions. Thicker gloves such as mitts are ideal for when it is very cold, and a thinner pair (commonly known as 'pipe gloves') is preferable for warmer days.

Off-Piste Equipment

Venturing into the 'backcountry' of the mountains and away from the patrolled, groomed slopes necessitates careful preparation and equipment selection. Commonly referred to as 'freeriding', snowboarders in search of fresh, untracked snow must be prepared to deal with a host of natural dangers. Snowboarders who are not suitably prepared with the appropriate equipment would put themselves at risk of falling victim to significant potential hazards, perhaps the most notorious and frightening of these being avalanches.

Near to the groomed runs, mountain resorts control avalanches with carefully detonated explosions, and it is common to hear the echoes of these explosions once the slopes are closed to the public. This tactic manipulates snowfall by setting off avalanches intentionally in order to secure safety around the pistes, a strategy which actually reduces the risk of an avalanche. However, freeriding still exposes a snowboarder to the risks of an uncontrolled, hostile terrain that has not been carefully prepped and primed for snowboarding. Fundamentally, the best way for a rider to guard against the natural dangers of freeriding is to choose the correct, specialized equipment for snowboarding off piste. Preparation is key. Although in the worst case scenario there is little that can be done against the awesome power and might of an avalanche, forward thinking and cautious planning is vital, and will enable a snowboarder tackling the backcountry to evade such dangerous situations, and equally as important, survive them.

A snowboarder heading into the backcountry must never do so unaccompanied, and it is prudent always to inform someone of your whereabouts and intended return. For the

Ben Kilner, venturing into the backcountry in Breckenridge. (© Nick Atkins)

Stewart Monk freeriding in Avoriaz, France. (© Nick Atkins)

Venturing off-piste requires specialized equipment. © Christian Brecheis, Ortovox

inexperienced snowboarder tackling freeriding it is highly recommended to be thoroughly prepared, and there are many specialized courses that an intrepid rider can attend in order to fully understand backcountry riding, its dangers, and how to use safety equipment correctly. Essential advice on survival for the rider, and life-saving techniques in the event of an avalanche, are hugely important. Entering the backcountry requires more than just a basic understanding of snowboarding, and an in-depth understanding of mountaineering and off-piste safety are imperative to the freerider.

The equipment required for freeriding and for avalanche safety are detailed below, and can be found in most snowboard shops.

Bag

A technical bag is essential for freeriding. It must be well fitting with adjustable waist and chest straps so that it won't bounce and so the snowboarder's movements are not restricted. It should have a shovel pocket on the front with straps to hold it in place, and further fastenings in order to hold other mountaineering tools, including probes and ice axes. There may be an opening to allow a water tube from a hydration pack. The material should be tough and hardwearing so as not to rip when loaded with equipment, but not too heavy in weight. It must also be waterproof so that your belongings or spare base layers do not get wet.

Transceiver

A transceiver is a signal send/receive device that is worn underneath the snowboard jacket. In the event of an avalanche the transceiver can be used in two ways: either to find a buried snowboarder, or to be found oneself. There are two signal settings, the default being the send signal so that you can be found when buried. With a flick of a switch the transceiver will be used to find the person/transceiver that is hidden.

Many outerwear brands have adopted 'Recco Chip' technology, which is commonly stitched into a snowboarding jacket. The detector is used to locate a buried person in an avalanche, but it is certainly no replacement for a transceiver,

Ortovox FreeRider backpacks feature numerous highlights, integrated SPS back protector, and a body-like silhouette so the close-fitting cut follows every movement without developing its own momentum. (© Christian Brecheis, Ortovox)

which offers a much stronger signal. Furthermore, ski patrollers searching for survivors in an avalanche will scan first for transceivers and secondly for Recco. The timeframe during a rescue mission following an avalanche is critical, because once a person is buried, the window frame to recover them alive is exceptionally tight. A buried snowboarder in possession of a transceiver will be picked up before a Recco signal, so it is advisable always to use a transceiver.

Bearing lines, direction arrow and distance information lead you along the fastest route to the strongest transmission signal/to the victim. (© Christian Brecheis, Ortovox)

Ortovox 3 plus a transceiver. The circular display allows you to focus on the essentials, namely the distance to, and the relative position of a victim. (© Christian Brecheis, Ortovox)

Probe

A probe is assembled much like a tent pole, in that it is made of many sections and joined together by a string. When searching for a body in an avalanche the probe is an essential part of the freerider's backcountry kit. It is constructed by joining together multiple rods to create a long stick, and pushed into the deep avalanche debris to find hard objects such as bodies.

The Ortovox probe is stretched within seconds. The individual segments have a diameter of 13mm, which makes the probe very stiff and thus accurate. The burial depth can be read easily to allow the planning of appropriate shovelling strategies. (© Christian Brecheis, Ortovox)

Shovel

A fold-up shovel is normally attached to the back of the rucksack. This indispensable item is not only used for digging in the snow to find bodies after an avalanche, it is also used to dig snow holes so that you can look at the different layers of snow to assess the avalanche risk before making a trek or a descent.

Ortovox shovel. The shovels are used in a mock avalanche rescue scenario. (© Christian Brecheis, Ortovox)

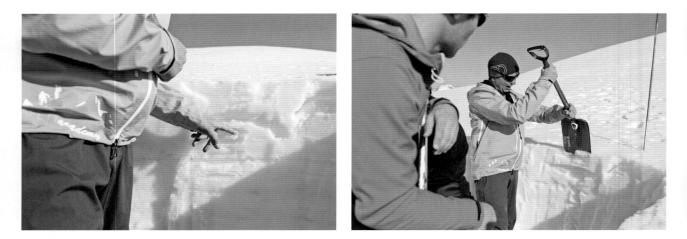

It is essential to check the impact on the different layers between the snow. (© Christian Brecheis – Ortovox)

An essential part of freeriding preparation is the scrutiny of snow layers. The snow on the mountain is made up of numerous layers, which will have fallen over a period of weeks or days. In between snowfalls the temperatures and weather can be highly changeable, which can have a major impact on the different layers between the snow. For example on sunny and warm days the top layer of the snow could have melted and then refrozen to create an icy, unstable layer. Fresh snow then settling on top of this frozen layer creates a high chance of an avalanche.

Digging out wedges with a shovel enables the freerider to make a logical assessment of the composition of the different layers, and the likelihood of any potential slides. The prudent freerider will thoroughly examine the snow conditions in this manner, and decide if they are safe enough to ride on.

Hydration Pack

Hydration is always a fundamental part of exercise, and when venturing deep into the mountains a snowboarder may not have the opportunity to access fresh drinking water. Carrying a bottle of water is possible, but if temperatures are very cold the bottle can freeze, or dig uncomfortably into a rider's back in the event of a fall. Numerous brands on the market offer hydration packs that are purpose built to fit readily into a backpack. The water chamber is a soft pouch that is insulated to keep the water

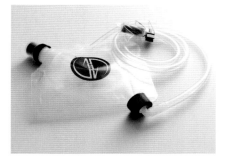

Travel flask.

either cold, or warm enough so that it does not freeze. There is often a tube that trails over the shoulder strap of the bag with an easy-seal nozzle, so that sips of water can be taken quickly and easily. Isotonic sports drinks are advisable as they hydrate the rider quickly, and contain high levels of sodium, which is lost in sweat precipitation. These can be purchased in ski shops as a powder form, which is an inexpensive way to fill your hydration pack.

High Energy Bars

Snowboarding is a fast-paced, energy-burning sport, and a quick way to replenish sapped energy on the mountain is by eating a sports bar. A mixture of simple carbohydrates and cereals (complex carbohydrates), a sports bar provides both fast and slow release energy. It is best to avoid ingesting heavy food before snowboarding as this is likely to weigh a snowboarder down significantly.

Snowshoes

A snowshoe is shaped rather like a tennis racket, and is fastened to a snowboard boot with a binding that is much the same as a snowboard binding. It is designed to disperse weight so that the wearer does not sink into deep, soft snow when walking. On the underside there are sharp teeth-like spikes that grip the ice to prevent slipping and sliding.

Snowshoes are not an essential item to carry, although hiking through deep snow can be difficult and tiring.

CHAPTER 6

SETTING UP YOUR SNOWBOARD

Stance

The first thing you must establish is whether you are a 'regular'- or a 'goofy'-footed snowboarder. 'Regular' riders stand with their left foot forward, and 'goofy' is the opposite, with the right foot used as the front foot. It is not the same as being right- or left-handed, and there is no proven way to find out which you are without actually trying. If you have experience of skateboarding or surfing, then you may already have a good idea as to whether you are a regular- or a goofy-footed snowboarder. The most straightforward way is to try simply by

standing on a snowboard with the help of an instructor. Once the basics have been learned such as a sideslip and falling leaf, try some turns as a regular snowboarder and then some as a goofy snowboarder. If you feel more at ease with one foot forward than the other, then the decision is made.

Once you have your board and you know which way you prefer to be

standing on it, lay it on the floor. However, note that there is always a recommended stance on a snowboard, which will be written on its top sheet.

Stand on your board with your feet on the bolts. If the recommended stance seems a little narrow, shuffle your feet out slightly and make a note of where you are standing – there is no right or wrong regarding the width of your

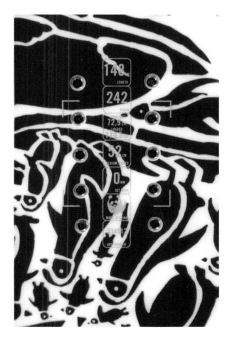

The recommended stance will be written on the top sheet of the snowboard along with other information about the board.

Example of a wide or 'fat' stance as compared to a narrow stance.

LEFT: Example of a racer stance.

BELOW: Example of binding angles set to +15 on the front foot and −15 on the back foot.

stance: it simply comes down to personal preference. A wide or 'fat' stance can offer more stability, but some find this to be uncomfortable. A narrow stance can be preferable for making quicker turns, although some feel that by having their feet so close together, they are raising their centre of gravity and feel unstable.

Most snowboarders have a fairly centred stance on the board, where the nose and tail are of equal length. This is fine, although sometimes as a beginner it may be a good idea to have the nose of

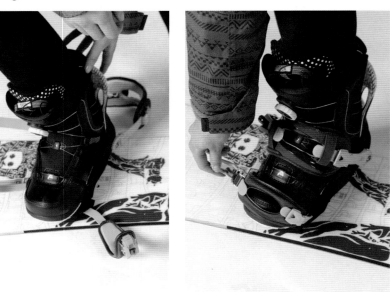

Check that the boot is pushed right to the back of the binding, and that the toe and heel overhang the snowboard edge by an equal amount.

your board slightly longer. This helps the rider to feel a little more secure when riding straight down the hill ('fall-line' snowboarding), as the longer nose will help to push through any bumps or soft snow that would normally risk throwing the rider off balance. At no point, however, should the tail be longer than the nose.

Angles

The next stage is to choose your binding angles. Racers have both feet pointing forwards as this avoids boot overhang on the narrow race boards, and is ideal for carving solid lines and holding maximum edge length while speeding down the mountain. However, as soon as you ride backwards (switch stance) it is useless.

The most common binding angles are set to +15 on the front foot and −15 on the back foot. This stance is called a 'duck foot' stance, and is ideal for riding both ways.

If the bindings are well fitted, they should need little to no adjustment. Place the binding over the snowboard bolt-holes and tighten lightly. Put the snowboard boot into the binding, checking that the boot is pushed right to the back of the binding. Look down from the nose of the board and check that the toe and heel overhang the snowboard edge by an equal amount. If the boot is overhanging on one edge more than the other, it would cause the snowboard to carve more heavily into one turn, and could cause the boot to drag in the snow. The binding position can be adjusted by using the different bolt-holes in the bindings base plate.

The forward lean can be adjusted to match your preference. Most people have enough forward lean so that they can feel it, but not enough to create discomfort. Generally the angle should be the same on both the front and back binding. Pipe riders tend to add a little more on the rear binding as this allows better performance when carving up steeper transitions.

Adjust your forward lean as shown.

Both front and back forward lean are set at the same angle.

Close-up of the forward lean.

CHAPTER 7

LOOKING AFTER AND SERVICING YOUR SNOWBOARD

As with all frequently used sports equipment, in time snowboards will suffer from general wear and tear. While snowboarding it is quite usual to ride over stones, rocks or even tree roots that are above the surface of the snow, which can cause considerable damage to a snowboard. Moreover the base material can wear dry from the friction caused from sliding on the ice and snow: noticeably the base becomes white in colour and has a rough or almost 'furry' feel to it. If it has been used in the snow park and on rails there will quite likely be digs, dents and scrapes in the base of the board from frequent contact with such obstacles.

If the scratches in the base of the board are deep and go right through to the core of the snowboard (known as a 'core shot'), this will allow moisture to penetrate the board, which will ultimately cause it to deteriorate and fray rapidly. Furthermore deep pits or scratches sustained to the base of the board can cause significant drag while snowboarding, affecting the overall performance of the board and rider.

The majority of specialist snowboard shops offer snowboard servicing, but general maintenance can easily be done at home. Substantial scrapes or visible damage to the edges of the board, or anything you don't feel comfortable doing yourself, may be better left to a specialist.

It is not essential to service a snowboard every time it is used, although a rider should keep an eye out for any damage that needs to be attended to. Edges only require sharpening intermittently, although the snowboard should be waxed more regularly. A high-level competitive snowboarder may wax their board each day before snowboarding so that the board always performs to its best, although this can become time-consuming. It is recommended that snowboards are waxed after every three or four days of riding, although it is not a problem to leave it for longer.

The Home Servicing Kit

Home service kits can be purchased that include most of the tools and equipment needed to fix or maintain a snowboard. The items required for home servicing are listed below.

Base Cleaner

A snowboard will accumulate old wax and ingrained dirt to its base, which will need to be removed prior to fresh wax being applied. Base cleaner should be evenly distributed across the base of the board and must be allowed time to soak in to lift dirt and break down old wax, before it is wiped clean. Common household solvents and spirits should not be used in place of a snowboard-specific base cleaner, as they can be damaging to the P-Tex base

All the equipment needed for servicing your snowboard.

material. Other water-based cleaners such as dish soap can be used, although recognized base cleaners offer the best performance.

Edge File

Snowboard edges can be described as the 'brakes' of a snowboard, and provide stability whilst turning. The edges are designed to cut sharply into the snow whilst turning, and after considerable use these edges can become blunt, and require sharpening. Edges can also sustain damaging nicks from coming into contact with stones; these nicks are commonly described as 'edge burrs'. Edge burrs need to be removed so that the edges can once more make a clean cut through the ice and snow.

P-Tex Strips

P-Tex is the material used to construct the base of a snowboard. There are two colour options, either clear or black. P-Tex can be melted and can then be used to fill deep cracks or scrapes in the snowboard base.

Wax

Snowboard wax is like a moisturizing cream for your snowboard base. It can be melted on to the base, when it soaks in to protect the P-Tex material, preventing the base from drying out and thereby

Snowboard wax.

affecting the board's performance. Snowboard wax improves the performance of the snowboard by helping it to glide quickly and smoothly across the snow.

Choosing the correct wax is a selective process as there are various options, dependent upon the condition of the snow on a given day. An experienced wax technician will take into consideration the temperature of the snow and humidity before selecting the apprpriate mixture of wax. Certain snowboard disciplines require different mixtures of wax, for example to enable the snowboard to accelerate faster or to provide improved glide stability at speed. For general snowboard maintenance it is best to select a universal, all-temperature wax. This is a comprehensive wax that works in any snow condition.

Wax Iron

A wax iron is used to melt and spread the wax on to the snowboard. Specialist snowboard wax irons do not differ greatly from other regular household irons, except that the metal base is smooth and the sides are rounded to encourage wax to spread. It is possible to use a household iron, however after using it to apply snowboard wax it will not be possible to use it for domestic ironing. Furthermore, the wax is likely to run and stick into the holes of a household iron, giving off smoke. The best option is to purchase a small travel iron that does not have holes for a steam function.

Plastic Scraper

When the wax has been applied and left to cool, the excess wax is scraped off and discarded. This is as important as waxing the board in the first place. As the wax is scraped off, wax is in turn pushed into the base and any damaged P-Tex is removed. It is not advisable to use a sharp metal scraper, which would scrape deeply against the base and could potentially damage the snowboard.

Finishing Brush

Snowboards are often factory produced with a base structure that improves the board's capacity to glide on wet snow. When wax is applied this structure is filled, so once the board has been waxed and scraped, the next step is to use an acrylic-haired brush to clear the wax from this base structure.

Step-by-Step Guide to Snowboard Maintenance Techniques

Allow the snowboard to become completely dry and warm to room temperature if it has been used prior to servicing. It is possible to purchase service clamps that will hold the snowboard in place while it is being serviced, but while this may make working easier, it is not essential. If working on a flat surface the bindings can be removed so that the snowboard will remain flat.

The first step in servicing a snowboard is to examine the edges of the board carefully. If there are burrs on the edges, these will need to be removed by using a pocket or diamond stone, a file that offers low abrasion and is found in a service kit. The stone is rubbed on the burrs to flatten them and to restore the edges of the snowboard.

Base-Side Edge

The edge file will only sharpen the side of the edge, and you can use the stone or remove the file from the edge file. Run the file smoothly from tip to tail while keeping the flat angle of the edge. Be careful not to damage or file the P-Tex base.

Side Edge

The edge files often have two sides with different file angles, where one side will hold an angle at 90 degrees, and the other at 89 degrees. 90 degrees would be the

standard option for general snowboarding, though if maximum edge grip or sharper edges for racing is desired, the 89 degrees option should be selected. By decreasing the edge angle a sharper point on the edge is created. Sharper edges will damage faster and may require more regular tuning. Take note that files only cut in one direction, and there is often a small arrow on the file indicating in which direction it should be used.

Set the file at the nose end of the snowboard (where the curve finishes), and make full, smooth passes over the edge with moderate pressure. Continue until the edge looks clean and even.

Detuning

Detuning comes down to personal preference, but the curved edge on the nose and tail of the snowboard should not be sharp otherwise it will catch and cause the board to perform poorly. The area of edge that is left sharp is known as the effective edge.

Run the file smoothly from tip to tail while keeping the flat angle of the edge.

The stone is rubbed over the burrs to flatten them.

Base Clean

Spread the base cleaner on to the snowboard and allow it to soak for five to ten minutes. The liquid draws the dirt and old wax to the surface so that it can be removed. With a dry cloth and a scraper, remove the old wax and wipe the board clean. This process can be repeated if necessary. The base should now look dry and pale in colour; once it has reached this stage it will be able to absorb the wax.

Repairing Deep Scrapes

Before fixing the holes in the base, the board should be warm and dry. Using a sharp blade, the damaged area should be scraped clean of excess dirt or loose plastic. Some small nicks should be made into the side of the hole so that the new P-Tex has something to bond to. The P-Tex can be melted in to the hole by setting fire to the strip. The first drips will be black with carbon residue, so use a

Set the file at the nose end of the snowboard (where the curve finishes) and make full, smooth passes over the edge with moderate pressure.

Heat the wax just enough so it drips on to the board.

Run a line of drips around the edges and then in a criss-cross through the middle of the snowboard.

Glide the iron up and down the snowboard to melt the wax evenly.

metal scraper to catch the drips until the burning P-Tex drips clear. Once the P-Tex has cooled, the excess or raised P-Tex can be cut or scraped off so that the hole is filled and the repair sits flush with the base of the board. A professional board technician will have a P-Tex gun, which is much like a glue gun and melts the P-Tex at the correct temperature; it will offer a cleaner finish. The boards are then often put through a base grinding machine to create a clean and flat base before waxing.

Waxing

Turn on the snowboard iron and allow it to heat. Some waxes will specify the required iron temperature, although a simple setting is for the iron to be hot

With the scraper, remove the wax from the nose of the snowboard to the tail.

iron moving so as not to melt or scorch an area. When the board is evenly covered and warm through, the job is done. Place the board somewhere safe to cool.

Scraping

Once the board has cooled back to room temperature, the wax can be scraped off. Holding the scraper with two hands (with the thumbs in the middle), push the angled scraper from the nose of the snowboard to the tail. Using the thumbs, flex the scraper to create a pressure point in the centre: like this the wax will roll off easily. By running a sharp plastic scraper across the base of the board, any rough or scorched P-Tex is removed and the wax is

pushed into the base, leaving the board fresh and shiny.

Brush

Run the brush from the nose of the snowboard to the tail. This may expose some areas of wax that have been missed or poorly scraped. The board should look revitalized, and the colours in the P-Tex should be as vibrant as they did when the snowboard was new.

enough to melt and spread the wax, but not so hot that it smokes, which would indicate that the wax is burning. Hold the wax to the iron so that it drips on to the board.

Only a small amount of wax is required to cover the base sufficiently – any excess wax will only be scraped off and wasted. Place the iron on the base of the snowboard and let it glide up and down so that the wax melts and is spread evenly. If it does not spread far enough to the edges, more can be added. Keep the

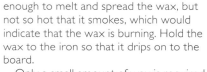

Finally brush to finish the snowboard.

PART 2

SNOWBOARDING TECHNIQUES

CHAPTER 8

APPROACHING THE SNOWBOARD PARK AND SNOWPARK GUIDELINES

The snow park can be an intimidating place for newcomers to the sport, a fast-paced environment habitually filled with many snowboarders and skiers quickly moving and changing direction. For a beginner snowboarder a few guidelines may help when entering the park for the first time.

Snow Park Guidelines

Before entering the snow park the newcomer would be wise to position himself somewhere where it is easy to view all the obstacles, and all the other riders in the park. That way, by observing others, he can begin to understand how the park works and how the snowboarders move through it. Before attempting to tackle any of the jumps or rails in the snow park, a snowboarder

People gather at the opening of the snow park.

Jamie Nicholls stands ready at the top of the park. (© Nick Atkins)

should have a ride through the park to see how big everything is in order to build an idea of what speed is required, and what is on the other side of any feature. Look before you leap!

A rider should take time to observe others, taking note of where they drop in from, and how many turns they make. A great deal can be learnt by paying attention to other riders in the park and carefully studying their movements. To prevent personal injury, a rider can learn from the mistakes of others – for example, if too much speed is used when approaching a kicker.

Those entering the snow park should be aware that there are various 'unwritten rules', which participants

Dan Wakeham with a clear landing. (© Nick Atkins)

observe in order to minimize the risk of accident. Many snow parks do in fact carefully list several rules at the entry to the park, many of which are the same as general mountain rules. More often they are common sense, but it is important to take note of them and to adhere to them when riding in a snow park:

- The elements in the snow park are only suitable for well trained winter sports athletes. A snowboarder should only use the jumps and rails they can manage easily.
- A rider is responsible for their own personal safety and that of the other skiers and boarders in the park. It is essential to be aware of other people, and to avoid riding dangerously or causing a hazard to oneself or others.
- It is important to control the direction and speed of travel, taking into account the terrain, snow, weather and traffic conditions.
- Select an appropriate path. If a snowboarder is riding behind someone, it is their responsibility to ride around without causing any danger.
- Before a rider starts or 'pulls out' towards a kicker or feature, they must look up and down the slope and choose an appropriate moment to execute their manoeuvre, so as not to endanger themselves or other mountain users.
- A rider can make others aware of them before dropping in by raising their hand or by saying 'dropping next'.
- A snowboarder should always avoid stopping at blind corners, when landing from a jump, or in narrow or enclosed places, unless they have to. In the case of an injury, the rider must vacate the spot as soon as is practicable, to avoid further danger (to themselves or others). Always stop at the side of the slope and never in the middle.
- The jump must be closed immediately if there is an accident, and the injured person stabilized and first aid provided (if known). Notify the ski

rescue team at the nearest lift station immediately.
- The side of the slope must always be used to walk up or down, whether with or without skis on.
- Before jumping, the snowboard park user must be sure that the landing is clear.

The mountain rules state that the rider or skier ahead has the right of way. It is the responsibility of the person behind to avoid them. This stands true in the snow park, but there are exceptions. A snowboarder must be careful not to break the flow of the snow park by stopping in front of every obstacle. If someone is in a run or is being filmed, appropriate space should be allowed to let them through.

If dropping in at the same time as someone, it is fair to say that the rider in front has priority, so the rider behind should slow down to give room to the snowboarder with priority. 'Snaking' is a term for people who jump the queue – snake or 'be snaked'. Of course the ideal is when people are polite and well mannered and wait their turn, but when adrenalin is added to the equation, people often lose patience. Often

people tend to hang around at the top of a jump or obstacle while they build their confidence, or wait for their friends to watch and film. If a rider does not want to wait for a friend and wants to go, they should pause for a second take in the surroundings, and if no one is moving, they should raise their hand and make it clear that they are about to go. This is not rude, it just comes back to the rule of 'not breaking the flow of the snow park'.

Everyone is considered equal regardless of their skill level, although snow park users should always have the correct equipment for use in the park. The snow park is for snowboarders and skiers with twin tip skis only, and is not a place for ski schools. If a rider believes that a ski school instructor is acting irresponsibly by bringing young children into the park, or someone is riding dangerously, they should not hesitate to report back to the park crew attendants.

It is a common occurrence for snowboarders to film or photograph each other in the park, although it is important to take time to think where to stand. A cameraman may hope to achieve the best angle, but he or she must be careful not to obstruct other snow park users.

Snow parks can be a hive of activity, so it is essential to be aware of other people and to avoid riding dangerously or causing a hazard to oneself or others.

CHAPTER 9

PARK OBSTACLES AND TRICKS

Most snow parks offer an array of features other than the standard jumps or rails. These are described below.

Rails

Many snowboard parks contain obstacles and features that closely resemble urban architecture – for example, stairs set with handrails or ledges. A rider can jump on these and slide to the bottom, in much the same way that a skateboarder would use these features in an urban city environment. Snowboard parks can contain an abundance of rails of different heights, widths and gradients, catering for different abilities, and furthermore whatever trick the rider may want to

Sean Miller, wall ride.

execute. A good snow park will contain a large selection of rails, offering the jibber snowboarder a wide choice.

Wall Rides

As might be surmised, this activity involves riding on a wall. These walls may be made of either plastic or wood, and can vary in size. Most often they have a transitioned snow ramp at the bottom. The idea is to slide up on to the wall, reach the top, and stop or stall before sliding back down.

Boxes

The original boxes mimicked rails or picnic benches. Straight boxes are ideal for learning rail tricks, as they are more stable. Now boxes come in all shapes and

Ed Gunn in a frontside board slide, Keystone, Colorado. (© Nick Atkins)

Dan Breen makes use of the boxes in a snow park.

Andrew Forwood taps a barrel in the park.

styles. Park designers try to be creative in designing challenging shapes with corners and kinks.

Jibs and Barrels

Jibbing is a term that is commonly used for a style of snowboarding that includes obstacles such as metal handrails, when the snowboarder would jump on them and slide along. Other features can be found in a snow park, which are designed to be tapped with the snowboard, or for the board to stall on top of them. Obstacles in a snow park may resemble urban objects, and the snowboarder has to think creatively as to which way these obstacles should be ridden.

Pole Jam

In a pole-jam set-up in a snowboard park a structure of metal poles is set vertically into the snow so a rider can use the obstacle much like a tree in natural terrain. The snowboarder can then jump up to tap the tree/pole, and use its resistance to spin off in a different direction. A pole jam can also be laid down at a lower angle, and the snowboarder can ride up and over the poles, and then across to the end. In skateboarding this feature is also known as a 'Wally bar', although in snowboarding it is often considerably bigger and is called 'cannons' or 'rocket rails', owing to the nature of the way a snowboarder rides quickly across the obstacle and 'shoots' off the other end into the air.

Hips, Spines or Corner Jumps

Hips, spines and corner jumps are all similar features in a snowboard park, although a corner jump is probably the best word to describe these features. The snowboarder rides straight off a steep jump but has to execute a turn in the air to finish with a landing that is at 90 degrees to the jump or take-off. With a hip or corner jump, a rider can only jump in one direction, whereas a spine jump has a landing on both sides.

Quarter Pipes

Quarter pipes are a similar structure to a halfpipe: they might be visualized as a halfpipe that has been halved again to leave just one remaining wall. The quarter pipes (QP) are also straight facing as to a sideways hit that you would find in the halfpipe. The snowboarder rides straight into the QP, launches off the lip into the air, and then lands in much the same place from which he or she took off. QPs are not a common feature to find in a snow park, as they break down quickly when ridden and are difficult to maintain. Events held on QPs are great crowd drawers, as the snowboarders are launched high into the sky while performing tricks. In 2007, Norwegian snowboarder Terje Haakonsen set the world record for the highest QP air: 9.8m high.

Technical Tricks

One of the main aims of freestyle snowboarding is the ability to perform technical tricks or stunts that are made to look as if they are performed with ease. Tricks include spins, flips and grabs, as described below.

Spins

When flying off a jump a snowboarder may choose to rotate the body to spin in the air. Each direction or axis has a different name.

Backside
For a regular rider, this would be turning to the right-hand side, and turning the back to the landing when leaving the jump.

Aimee Fuller going huge over a hip in Les Deux Alpes. (© Nick Atkins)

Ben Kilner cranks out a huge backside aircranks out a backside air. (© Nick Atkins)

Baptiste Prost frontside air, Avoriaz, France. (© Nick Atkins)

Frontside

A frontside spin is the opposite direction to a backside spin, and is executed by opening the shoulders to face the landing when leaving the jump.

The spins would then be repeated switch. Switch backside is recognized as being the hardest direction to spin. Switch frontside is known as 'spinning Cab', a term derived from skateboarding. Steve Caballero was the inventor of the skateboarding trick, and it has remained as a snowboard trick name.

Rotations are measured by the number of degrees, which increase at 180 degrees at a time. A full rotation would be a 360. It is common to see spins such as a 1,080 in competition, although Norwegian rider Ulrik Badertscher performed the biggest spin ever landed, a 1,620, which is four and a half rotations. When a snowboarder spins on to a rail or box, the rotations slightly differ in degrees as the rider is able to land sideways in a board slide position. With this you get a 270 or a 450 spin on to, or off a rail or box.

Spins then can have a different axis, either flat, where the body position is totally upright, or off axis, commonly known as a 'corkscrew'. The snowboarder would spin sideways in the air and follow a rotation much like a metal corkscrew bottle opener, hence the name.

It has become extremely common to see a 'double cork' performed in competitive snowboarding. This is much like the rotation of a corkscrew, but in addition the rider goes upside down twice. At the cutting edge of competitive freestyle snowboarding, people are starting to spin triple corks, which is very impressive, although some consider that these tricks have become too gymnastic and with the fast rotations needed to perform these tricks, style is compromised.

Flips or Inverts

Flips include the basic front and backflip, but they can be mixed in with spins to create other tricks. For example, a backflip mixed with a backside 540 is known as a 'backside rodeo'. An invert can describe any trick where the snowboarder's feet go above the head.

Jack Shackleton performing a backside rodeo. (© Nick Atkins)

Grabs

A mid-trick whilst in the air, the snowboarder grabs the board to demonstrate style and control. The board can be grabbed anywhere, and there is a long list of names – some are self explanatory, such as nose and tail, but others can be quite obscure, such as 'stalefish' or 'chicken salad'. Most names come from skateboarding originally. When the board is grabbed, the body can become twisted or a leg straightened to add style. This is known as 'tweaking'.

A 'shifty' is a trick without a grab. The legs are twisted into the start of a rotation, but the upper body remains straight so that the legs can be brought back in line for the landing. This movement often happens in other tricks to add style or to reduce the distance between the board and the arm. For example, if a snowboarder wanted to grab the tail end of the board with the front hand, he or she would need to twist the board so that the back leg was closer to the front hand.

Over the years variations of the grabs and their tweak directions seem to go through trends, but described below are some of the most common grabs (with a regular rider in mind).

Indy
To execute an 'indy' grab, the right hand grabs the snowboard in between the legs. It can be tweaked by extending either the front or rear leg to result in an indy nose or tailbone. Mostly in snowboarding, the right arm should be inside the back knee, although in skateboarding the favoured style would be for the arm to reach round the outside of the knee. This is known as a 'tuck knee indy'.

Method or Mellon
The left hand grabs the heel side edge behind the legs. If the tweak is pushed out in a forward direction and the board kept flat underfoot, the grab is known as a 'mellon' grab. However, if the board is pushed into a backside shifty, or is tilted up behind the rider, it is known as a 'method'.

Dan Wakeham performs an indy grab. (© Nick Atkins)

Dan Wakeham performs a truck driver.

Gien Simmen, Stalefish, Laax.
(© Nick Atkins)

Stalefish

When leaving the jump, a frontside 90-degree shifty is performed to allow the right arm adequate space to reach down behind the legs to grab the heelside edge of the snowboard in a stalefish.

Mute

Much like an indy, a mute is grabbed on the frontside edge, but this time with the left hand.

Truck Driver

Like a truck driver who holds on to the steering wheel with both hands, the truck driver grab is a mixture of an indy and a mellon grab. If tweaked to the side (which is hard) the trick is known as a 'drunk driver'.

Gorilla Grab

By combining both an Indy and a mute grab, a snowboarder's body position could resemble that of a gorilla with knuckles on the floor and knees out to the sides.

Japan Air

Essentially a Japan air is a mute grab, although the arm reaches round the outside of the front knee and is tilted up and pulled in tightly to fully bend the front knee (tuck knee).

Although each rider is free to grab where he or she likes, in competition there are certain areas on the board that many consider to be forbidden grabs. This is the area between the back foot and the tail on either rail. The toe-edge grab which is not an indy and not a tail but a mix of both is named the tindy. On the heelside edge, the area

Dan Wakeham performs a mute tailbone.

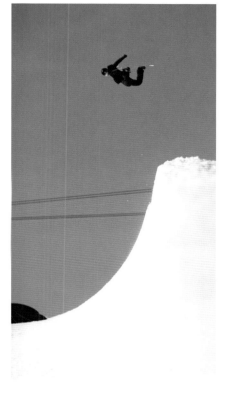

*Ben Kilner doing a Japan air, Laax.
(© Nick Atkins)*

which is neither a stalefish nor a tail grab
is named a tailfish.

These are often the first grabs
performed by beginner snowboarders as
they are simple, but they are also
considered to be bad style.

Handplants

'Handplants' is the name given to a trick
that once more is derived from
skateboarding. The skateboarder would
stall on the top of the ramp on their
hand before landing back on the ramp on
their board. It is the same on a
snowboard, although with a board
strapped to the snowboarder's feet
(unlike a skateboard) he or she is able to
balance in more challenging places, such
as on top of a wall ride.

Dom Harrington-styled handplants. (© Nick Atkins)

CHAPTER 10

DISCIPLINES IN DEPTH: BIOMECHANICS AND THE HALFPIPE

In this chapter we delve a little deeper into the disciplines and look at techniques that could speed or aid your progression.

Biomechanics

An understanding of biomechanics in snowboarding may help you analyse and think about your movements in snowboarding, or how a trick is performed correctly. Where there is an action, there is a reaction.

This could lead you into thinking about hitting a jump – or any obstacle, for that matter. It is not always as simple as just riding off a huge jump, turning your head and expecting your body to spin a 1,080-degree rotation. The spin would need to be initiated before leaving the jump and then terminated at landing. As soon as you have lost your edge on the jump and you are in the air, there is little you can do to change your spin direction. While snowboarding, small adjustments in body position could be the difference between a move or trick working, or not at all.

Sequence of a 50/50 grind. In its most basic form, grinding in snowboarding is mostly just riding over anything that is not snow. The most fundamental move is the 50/50 grind.

When professional snowboarders work with a coach this is something they look out for. Video analysis is used so that the athletes can see for themselves what is required in their technique to correct the movements, so that a trick flows naturally and with ease. This is considered to be 'good style'.

There are common rules of physics that affect snowboarding in motion. Your snowboard direction generally follows the direction of your head. For example, if you look to the left, your shoulders will in turn follow, as will your hips and then legs. With this in mind, you should be looking where you are going, not at your feet. Remember that your knees are your suspension: if you ride with stiff legs at high speed and hit a bump, your board will leave the ground.

The body position of a snowboarder performing a backside 3.

The Halfpipe

Halfpipe riding is one of the most technical disciplines in snowboarding. The snowboarders have to ride smoothly and with clean lines to ensure that they can keep the speed for a run of around five to six high airs. Any small mistakes can ruin the whole run.

The Olympic standard for halfpipe construction is 120–165m in length, 20m in width, and on a slope angle that is 17.5–18.5 degrees. The walls then stand 6.7m in height.

The basic halfpipe foundations are often dug into the ground in the summer time so that less snow is needed for the giant ice construction. New wet snow is generally the best snow to work with, as it bonds together well and then freezes into shape. Early in the season in North America, temperatures are often cold with low amounts of humidity in the air. This allows the halfpipe to be built with artificial snow. This type of snow is expensive but has the best longevity, and often sets for a good solid base without ice layers or air pockets.

Building a good halfpipe takes a lot of careful and scrupulous planning. To be successful, the project needs experienced shapers who are patient and pay attention to detail. The snow for the pipe walls is pushed together and then cut into steps. The shapers then use a huge curved

Halfpipe at the glacier in Kitzsteinhorn, Kaprun.

A Zaugg pipe monster in action shaping a pipe.

cutting device called a Zaugg pipe monster, looking much like a farming tool or curved plough with a rotating blade. They then proceed to make runs up and down the pipe, each time taking away only a small amount of snow. It is a long, slow process but is considered to be an art. The final result will be a clean, smooth transition with the peak of the angle between 83 and 88 degrees.

A south-facing halfpipe will be slightly more hospitable for the general public as the sun will soften the walls during the day, making it a little safer and less intimidating. A north-facing halfpipe can be good for professionals, as the walls will remain firm and icy. Icy walls are good because they offer the riders consistency, although a north-sloping pipe would regularly have low light conditions so is best built in an area with either trees or floodlights.

When riding the pipe to a high level, the snowboarder has to put trust in the pipe wall so that he or she knows that the wall will send them in the right direction. If the rider were to drift away from the wall, he or she could expect a very heavy or flat landing, while to drift the other way could result in them hitting the coping or deck, with potentially dangerous consequences.

With this in mind, a resort that plans to hold a world-class event would need to put a lot of planning and money into building the right feature. As a pipe rider in Europe you would expect to travel to find the best pipes, just like a surfer travels to find the best waves. The USA generally boasts the best pipes in the world, and the resorts pride themselves in what they have to offer and how well they are maintained. As the pipes have grown over the years, the riders' choice of snowboard has had to be adapted to meet the need for better edge grip and added speed.

With bigger, longer wall transitions, riders have been able to gain more height and air, allowing more time for technical tricks, flips or rotations. It is now not uncommon to see double flips or big rotations such as a 1260, which is four body rotations.

Halfpipe Basics

Before entering the halfpipe, it helps if you have prior knowledge of edge control, or an idea of how to carve. If you feel intimidated by an icy morning pipe, take a few runs and come back when the sun has softened the walls.

Entering the Pipe

The process of entering the pipe is called 'dropping in' (as in skateboarding). In some halfpipes you will be able to start in the centre of the pipe with little speed, and then work your way up. Other resorts choose to put a net across the centre or the drop-in area, because they feel that if you cannot drop in on a transitioned wall, then your skill level is not high enough to ride the halfpipe. This is not just aimed at beginner snowboarders: it is to stop the ski schools going through the middle, creating bumps and damaging the walls.

The easiest side to drop in on will be on the toe edge. If you are regular, this will be the left-hand side as you look down the pipe. The right-hand side is for goofy footers. As you stand on the edge of the halfpipe, shuffle your board forwards so that the nose is overhanging the drop. When you feel ready, push your

Aimee Fuller drops in.

weight on to the nose of the board so that you slip in. The idea is to match the angle of your body to the angle of the wall. If you lean too far back or too far forwards, the chances are that you will fall.

As you enter the halfpipe you should come on to your toe edge, with your head up and looking where you are going. Your knees should be bent and your body position should be like a ninja, low and ready for anything. You shouldn't worry about pumping, you should just concentrate on getting to the bottom of the pipe in control.

For riders who plan to drop into the pipe with maximum speed, which is a more advanced drop-in, the approach into the pipe entry is a little different. You should ride in a straight line parallel to the coping of the halfpipe. The safest way is to get as close to the edge as possible and then roll in, keeping a long, curved line. If you make too steep a turn into the pipe, the chances are that you will fall to the flat bottom.

Frontside Air

If you have mastered the drop-in, the chances are that you will be flying across the flat bottom of the halfpipe and rapidly approaching a steep, icy wall. As you reach the wall you should shift your weight on to your back leg. Notice that I say 'shift your weight', and not 'lean back', because if you lean back, you will initiate a back flip. Your weight should still be 100 per cent on top of your board, but divided to 60 per cent on your back leg and 40 per cent on your front. This allows your board to ride smoothly up the wall and at a consistent pace. If you have too much weight on your front leg, your board will crash into the wall and your weight will be pushed forwards, sending you out of control.

The next step is to think about your body position. Your board generally follows delayed movements from your shoulders, so it is often a wise idea to point with your lead hand in the direction that you plan to follow. Think about the line that you hope to describe: if your front shoulder is dropped, you will not achieve the arc turn needed. On the way up, you should be looking up and pointing towards the halfpipe lip (coping). As you start to reach the peak of your speed, and as your weight starts to change the direction of gravity from up to down, you will need to think about changing your lead hand to point down the hill to initiate the turn.

At this point you should aim to do a little jump with enough height to allow your board enough free space to turn. With this jump you should be thinking about coming from your toe edge on to your heel edge. As soon as you touch down, your concentration and point hand should be aimed at the opposite wall.

Advanced Frontside Air

The advanced frontside air is an air where you leave the top of the halfpipe. The approach will be much the same as before, just with added speed. Half pipes vary in steepness, so it is wise to work towards getting out of the pipe gradually – that way you will have an idea or feeling of the pipe's steepness. As you get higher up the wall, you will need to do less of a jump as the steepness will do most of the work for you. You can grab your board wherever feels comfortable, by bringing your knees into your chest and extending your arm – although at first it may be safer to keep your arms up for balance and stability in the air.

You should now be looking back into the halfpipe and concentrating on putting you board back down on to the snow. You should be ready either to bend or extend your legs to place your board on to your heel edge as high to the top of the transition as possible. As you drop down into the pipe, your legs should come underneath you nicely. As you travel across the flat bottom, you should keep a clean line without changing edges. The idea is to keep your speed up so that you can maintain a consistent height out of the halfpipe on each hit.

Kevin Pearce drops into the pipe toe edge. (© Nick Atkins)

Backside Air

The next step is to learn a backside air. This is generally harder at first than the frontside air because the knees only bend one way. When you are stood on your toe edge your knees bend over the toe, which is perfect for stability and as suspension. You are naturally better balanced while stood on your toes. On your heel edge it is a little harder, but it is a technique that needs to be worked on.

As with the frontside air, many of the techniques are the same. The shoulders should be square, and your lead arm should be guiding your chosen direction. Your weight should be shifted on to your back leg and your body position should be low, bent at the knees with a straight back.

As you start to ride up the wall you will find that you have to fight the urge to drop your lead arm early. If you do, the arc of the turn will be too long and you will not reach the top of the pipe.

Try to hold your line as you go up the wall. If you find that you slip or skid, this could be the result of a line that is too straight or steep up the wall. Try to add more downhill angle and bend your

knees. If the problem persists you could sharpen the edges of your snowboard for a sharper cut on the ice, or add more angle to the forward lean on your bindings – this will encourage your knees to bend a little more and make your board respond more quickly.

Keep looking up towards the top of the pipe until your weight starts to change direction. This time you will have to think about hopping from your heel edge to landing on your toes. As with landing from the frontside air, you should again keep a clean line, staying on your toe edge to travel across the flat bottom of the halfpipe, being low and ready for the next air.

As your pipe riding progresses, your main aim will be to gain as much height as you can out of the pipe. Pipes change from one resort to another, and there are many different techniques that work for different halfpipes: this is something that comes with experience. Most often it will be as simple as changing the steepness of your line up the halfpipe wall.

One of the best ways to build up speed is by pumping. This is a technique that you will know if you have ever ridden a ramp on a skateboard. A basic explanation is this: as you rise up a transition, you lift and swing your weight up (much like jumping); and as you start to drop back down the transition, push your weight down on to the board. This will provoke an accelerating effect, therefore gaining more speed for bigger airs.

As a pipe rider you should have an energetic style. It is not as simple as many make it look. You should be low, ready and aggressive. Pipe riding is one of the hardest disciplines to master, but it teaches you to snowboard to the best possible level.

Waxing and board servicing are an important aid in top-level pipe riding. This is not because it is a race, rather because it is necessary to hold your speed for big airs, and then to gain speed to cover up mistakes.

Gian Simmen, backside air at the Burton European Open 2011. (© Nick Atkins)

CHAPTER II

SNOWBOARD CROSS (SBX)

Snowboard cross is always extremely popular in televised events. For the snowboard cross rider there is no need to be able to do tricks or to demonstrate style: it is all about courage, going fast and taking chances. Some courses are extremely challenging, with 30m and sometimes even larger jumps. The X-Games courses always stand out as some of the most exciting runs, with the biggest and most dangerous and challenging of features.

As a newcomer to SBX, you really have to be aware of what is going on in the immediate surroundings of such a place, and to remember that first and foremost the snowboard cross track is a racecourse. Before dropping in, the snowboard cross racer should take a moment to give potentially slower racers a chance to clear the way. The rider should make an observation of the people on the course. If it is a snowboard cross rider's first run or first attempt, they may want to inform other riders on the course that they will be riding through it slowly in order to assess it carefully and to get to grips with the turns and jumps.

If a snowboard cross racer were to fall on their run, it is essential that they get back on to their feet as soon as possible and clear the way, as the fast-paced, aggressive course is ridden by other snowboarders. In most resorts the SBX course will be relatively safe, containing no big jumps, as the resort managers do not want the general public to risk injury. The jumps are more like banked slaloms. This

is not necessarily detrimental to a course, as to be the fastest racer down the course, a rider has to choose the cleanest and fastest line.

A snowboard cross racer visiting a European glacier in the autumn will find fewer members of the general public on the mountain, and more serious skiers and snowboarders in the resort, so there is a very good chance that a well built SBX track will be found. Many national teams choose this time of the season to do their most serious training. Such a course is likely to contain larger jumps or other dangerous obstacles that may not be built into the SBX course used by the general public in peak season. If there are national teams training and there is a coach at the start gate, a rider should not hesitate to ask them if there is anything in the course that they should look out for.

Snowboard cross is a real test of a snowboarder's standard. It is designed to challenge the rider's ability to stay in control, and although a well made track should be ridden with few or no speed checks, a snowboarder should ride

cautiously until they confidently recognize each corner or jump.

Snowboard Cross Equipment

In professional snowboard cross competitions, body armour and helmets are mandatory, and this is for good reason. The SBX track can be extremely dangerous, and the majority of racers wear padded shirts, impact shorts, back protectors and full-face helmets, all of which are not so different from those worn by motocross riders.

The best boards as required for SBX racing cannot be bought in shops, but are custom made by hand, and mostly produced by the brand Kessler. The boards cost around €1,300, and are only used for competition or training. They are long and stiff with extremely fast black graphite bases. The nose and tail are short with very little rise, and with no base graphics. The board must be as fast as possible, as it is all about cutting

Zoe Gillings at the Snowboard Cross World Cup in Switzerland. (Courtesy @zoegillings)

Zoe Gillings pops out from the start at the Winter X Games. (Courtesy @zoegillings)

seconds. The usual dye-cut P-Tex bases found on freestyle snowboards are said to cause drag.

The boards use a special base structure, which on close inspection resembles a cross-hatch effect. This design is all about displacing the moisture in the snow to cut down friction. The riders may have more than one board, which are structured differently for either wet or dry snow conditions.

Waxing is also a key part of cutting seconds. SBX teams travel with wax technicians, so it is not uncommon to see someone with a thermometer measuring the temperature of the snow. The technicians often set up their workstations by the start gates. They will have a selection of waxes and small pots of powders, for which you could expect to pay €150. The powders are not wax, but 100 per cent fluorinated carbons. The raw material is of the purest quality, and specifically synthesized for racing bases. The idea is to create the maximum amount of glide on top of the snow.

A technician's other tools would include corks, for rubbing in the powders – the cork creates enough friction to melt the fluros into the base – also a selection of

brushes of different stiffness, and a round brush attached to a cordless drill, used to clear the wax out of the base structure.

SBX Training

When SBX teams train, they often divide the track into sections so they can meticulously learn each feature. This is a good idea for practice, but entering a racetrack mid-way can be dangerous, so a rider must be sure to start from an area with a clear view.

The fastest SBX racer will have closely studied the track. They often film a run with a helmet camera, then watch it back on a large screen in the evening. As with any race sports, the start is one of the most important parts of the race. As the bar drops, the racer must be first out of the gate otherwise it can be extremely difficult to pass opponents. The racers often spend time working on their start and their pull-out technique.

Riding Position and Technique

The best riding position in snowboard

cross is a very low stance, in order to be prepared for any bumps and jumps. This is also the most aerodynamic position that the racer can be in.

When entering a corner – or as it is known in SBX, a 'berm' – the best way to maintain maximum speed is to get high into the bank early on, and keep a clean line until the exit. This can vary from corner to corner. Bumps or rollers are used to maximize speed by the pumping technique: as the racer rises over the peak of a bump they should be light on the board, or even pre-jump; then as the board reaches the downside of the bump, the racer should push heavily on to the nose, causing the board to accelerate. Occasionally it is possible to see the rider's gap over the bumps, as they would be going too fast to pump.

If a snowboarder were hitting a jump as a freestyle rider, they would pop (jump) and grab – but the SBX racer would try to do the opposite. The correct technique for hitting a jump is to be as aerodynamic as possible. When leaving the jump, the knees should be compressed so that the snowboarder rides through the curved transition of the kicker. The jump trajectory should be long, not high, and the body position should be tucked up like a ball. If the racer were to fall or make a mistake in the run, he or she would nevertheless be wise to continue, as the predictability of the race is always uncertain.

During the gold medal final of the SBX at the 2006 Winter Olympics, American World Cup SBX leader Lindsey Jacobellis was approaching the end of the course with a 43m, 3sec lead over Tania Freiden of Switzerland. On the final jump she decided to 'show off' and do a styled-out grab to claim her medal – but somehow she managed to twist her body position in the air and was unable to pull it back, resulting in a crash, and Freiden passed her to win the gold. Jacobellis recovered and took the silver. It was a very exciting race, and demonstrates the unpredictability of SBX.

CHAPTER 12

RAIL RIDING AND BOXES

Rail Riding or Jibbing

Snowboarding also has an urban side to it, much like skateboarding, which uses the streets. Rail riding is common in countries such as Canada, particularly in Quebec, where the cities are full of snow in the winter: there is no need to buy a lift pass when the snow is on the doorstep. The only issue that the urban snowboarders find is how to get speed. A skateboarder's legs are unstrapped, allowing them the ability to push, whereas for snowboarding, a hill or run-in is necessary in order to build up speed. Inner-city snowboarders construct drop-in ramps, which they then cover with snow.

In recent years it has become popular to use a snowboard-specific bungee cord, which is tied to a lamp-post, stretched out by a peer, and handed to the snowboarder who is then propelled forward at a rapid pace. These bungee cords can pull the snowboarders at 30mph, and have really revolutionized urban snowboarding. They also allow snowboarders to ride terrain that was previously unusable because it was impossible to generate enough speed.

Snowboard parks in resorts try to imitate urban features by building obstacles such as a stair set with multiple handrails or ledges for the snowboarders to ride on. In flatter terrain such as in the UK, Holland and Belgium, snow domes have appeared all over the place. In these domes, rails and boxes are very common features as they need little snow and little maintenance, whereas building a jump or kicker in a dome would be a major construction.

Milton Keynes Xscape snowdome. Whitelines snowboarding magazine organized a longest rail grind at the dome, which saw Calum Paton break the world record with 78.70m on 2 December 2011.

Jamie Nicholl's frontside board slide, street rail, Frisco, Colorado. (© Nick Atkins)

Hitting a Box

Most snow parks contain a wide selection of rails and boxes that suit each skill level. The easiest way to learn how to ride rails is to start on a low, wide box. The main thing that a rider needs to remember is that they have to be able to ride in a straight line from start to finish, because when riding the box, the snowboarder must be committed to ride it out until the end. There is no option to turn or stop because the rider will be sliding quickly on plastic.

It is wise to observe others who are riding the feature in order to get an impression of the speed required in the approach, and in order to ride across it completely. It is always a good idea to set a straight line early so there is time to prepare the body position. As always, the rider should be kept up, looking towards the end of the box. It is also helpful to point to the end of the box with the lead hand, and to maintain this position until landing.

As the snowboarder rides on to the box, the base of the board must be kept flat; if he turns on to an edge, it is likely that the board will slip out. Common mistakes at this point would be to turn on the box before the end: this would result in the snowboarder landing sideways and possibly catching an edge.

As the end of the box is reached, the body position should still be low. Drop off the box landing straight, find control and ease the speed.

Hitting a Rail

Snowboard rails come in numerous widths and gradients, and involve different ways of actually getting on to the rail. Easier rails will entail jumping straight on, whereas the more challenging and steeper, advanced rails require the snowboarder to jump on to the side of the rail in order to ride across it.

Rails are thin and metal, so riding them requires considerably more control than riding a box feature. When riding a wide box, the rider will have room to drift to

Although rails are traditionally made of metal, there are several things you can use in nature in the same way, such as large fallen trees, logs or smooth-edged rocks. Here, Stefani Nurding makes use of a fallen tree in Slovenia. (© Penny Cross)

Baptiste Prost hits a box in Avoriaz. (© Nick Atkins)

Jamie Nicholls grabs over a rail. (© Nick Atkins)

Andy Nudds, Kaunertal, 2012.

the sides, whereas with a rail, you must remain perfectly straight and centred on the rail: drifting to the side will result in the rider slipping off the rail early and probably falling.

Approach the rail with adequate speed to reach the end with ease. As with the box, concentrate on looking and pointing to the end of the rail. If you have to jump straight on to the rail, be sure to lift the knees so the board can be lightly placed on the rail.

For a side-on jump the approach is slightly different. The safest way to approach the rail is so that it is in directly in front: the key is finding the correct approach angle. If the rider comes into the rail at too steep an angle, they will slip off the other side when they jump on, whereas not enough of an angle will result in the rider slipping back off the side they

jumped on. A gentle angle is needed without getting too close to the rail itself.

Also, enough space must be left for the rider to jump and place their board on to the rail; they must take into consideration the steepness of the rail. The body angle must be matched so as not to fall back.

Once on a rail, however the rider has launched themselves on to it, the experience will be much the same. As with the box, there is no option to change

your speed or direction, although while balancing on a round rail it is possible to lean the board from side to side to straighten your line. Again, when coming off the rail, the knees should be bent to absorb the drop. Edge control should be found, and then the speed eased.

Laura Berry, Rogla, Unitur Ski Resort, Slovenia. (© Penny Cross)

Stefani Nurding hits a rail in Rogla, Unitur Ski Resort, Slovenia. (© Penny Cross)

CHAPTER 13

BIG AIR AND JUMPS

'Big air' is a one-hit display of snowboard skill and talent. The rider speeds down a steep run-in and hits a carefully built jump of snow, which propels them into the air.

At this point the big-air rider performs technical flips, spins and grabs before landing on a steep hill, which is normally about 20m away from the jump. As with riding the halfpipe, the riders are judged on their style and control, and the technical difficulty of their performance. Once more, emphasis is then placed on the overall impression and the ease with which the trick is performed.

During a big-air competition the snow conditions can change rapidly, and the snow can become faster or slower as the temperature changes. The rider must stay observant of these changes for his or her safety. Big air can be dangerous because the riders travel into the jumps at speeds of 40–50mph and then boost high into the air. An error of judgement of speed could result in the rider either bouncing off the top flat or the knuckle (the rounded area where the top flat meets the steep landing area), or if they are going too fast, missing the landing altogether, when they will literally fall from the sky.

Big-air events have become very common in inner-city environments, where the drop-in, take-off and landing can be built in scaffolding and then covered in artificial snow. The artificial snow is formed by forcing water and pressurized air through a specially designed machine called a snow cannon. Normally, cold temperatures are required, although with inner-city jumps they use big tents to hold the snow and create a microclimate.

A rider lands on the knuckle (the rounded area where the top flat meets the steep landing area) at the London Freeze snowboarding event.

ABOVE AND RIGHT: The London Freeze, a snowboarding and live music event held at Battersea Power Station. The drop-in, take-off and landing are built from scaffolding.

Artificial snow is expensive and uses a lot of water, so these events require considerable investment. However, the use of artificial snow allows for events to be held in cities such as London, where snow is a rare occurrence. The snow lasts well, although can be destroyed quickly if it starts to rain.

Dan Wakeham at the London Freeze 2008 event held at Battersea Power Station. (© Penny Cross)

The view from the top of the scaffolding at London Freeze 2008.

Hitting a Jump

As with trying anything new, it is wise to start small and work up to bigger cbstacles. The basics of hitting a jump are similar to hitting a rail or box, in that the rider must ride straight on to the jump; once the jump is left there is little that can be done to correct the speed or direction. The beginner will find it hard to judge the correct speed needed to clear the top flat area and land cleanly on the down side, and it is wise to watch other park users to get an idea of the jump's steepness, and the trajectory and speed needed. Once you have a clear idea of what is needed in terms of speed, head on to join the queue. While waiting for a turn, the rider should always be watching others to monitor any changes in snow speed as the temperatures change. When ready, the rider should raise their hand so that people know that they intend to drop in next.

On the run-in to the jump, the rider should aim to ride straight with gentle turns to get rid of excess speed. The easiest way to leave a kicker is with the bodyweight slightly on the toes. When approaching, the snowboarder should ride on to the heels or to the left-hand side of the jump for regular riders, and then when reaching the transition of the jump, the board should roll gently on to the toe edge. The rider should always be looking and pointing off the end of the jump and to where they hope to land. You should not jump (pop) when leaving the jump. The knees should be bent, and you should try to ride through the transition or whip of the jump, much as an SBX rider would.

The reason for this is so that if you have misjudged your speed you will not be too high in the air, which will lessen the chance of injury. As soon as you are in the air you will have a good idea as to whether you

have misjudged your speed, but at this point there is nothing you can do. In these circumstances you should try to remain calm and relaxed. One way to soften the impact of a heavy landing is to aim to land tail first. The flex of your board will help to ease you into the impact.

If your judgement has been correct, then you should stay relaxed with arms up next to the body to create a stable body position. As you come in to land, you will have to either extend or bend the legs to reach the landing. As the board touches down on the landing you should

Jamie Nicholls takes off heelside on a kicker. (© Nick Atkins)

Peetu Piiroinen, Laax, Switzerland. (© Nick Atkins)

remain straight and continue looking to the bottom of the landing while bending your knees to absorb the impact. After riding through the full landing, control the speed and move safely away from the landing zone so you are not in the way of other users of the jump.

Once a jump has been ridden confidently for a while, you will learn the speed and the feeling of a controlled flight, and you will start to feel more comfortable and relaxed. At this point you can think about adding more pop and experiment with grabs.

To add more pop you simply stiffen your legs as you ride up the transition of the jump. This will encourage your bodyweight to continue the direction of the jump trajectory. To grab the board you must simply bring your knees into your chest while in the air, bringing your board to your hand. Do not be tempted to reach down or bend over to grab your snowboard, as this would cause you to lose your balance in the air.

The most common simple grab for a beginner is an 'indy' grab. To execute an indy grab, the rider grabs the front edge of the board with their backhand in between their feet.

Spinning

After experimenting with various grabs, you may feel confident and ready to try a spin. Experiment while riding on a slope with a gentle incline: jump around in both directions, and first try 180s and 360s. Some people find that they have a natural spinning direction and one way is easier. For many, the most natural direction is to spin backside.

When it comes to attempting a spin on a jump, remember that a 180 will mean that you will have to land backwards, or 'switch'. Your switch riding will need to be of a good enough standard to ride at a considerable speed down a steep landing slope. The spin will need to be initiated on the kicker, but the timing is essential: too early and you will risk either catching an edge on the jump or drifting off to the side; too late and you may not have

Nelson Pratt, doing a Michalchuk in Les Deux Alpes. (© Nick Atkins)

enough push from your board on the snow to complete the full rotation. To get the correct line for a spin on a jump, your track or line should resemble an 'S' shape.

Backside Spin

With the intention of spinning backside, the approach to the kicker should be slightly to the right-hand side of the jump. Near to the bottom you will switch on to your heel edge and drift to the left-hand side of the jump. Half way up the jump come on to your toes and come towards the centre. By doing this, you are preloading your body for a rotation. The arms should be loaded and held back ready to swing. Just as you are about to leave the jump, swing your arms and turn your shoulders. Take into consideration that you are on an angled take-off. Your arms should stay level when swinging: if they do not, your spin will not be flat and will be more like a corkscrew.

In the air you should keep your body tight and balled up. Your head should remain upright, and looking over your leading shoulder in the direction that you are spinning. As you spot the landing, this should become your focus point. At this point you can open your body to slow the spin and extend your legs to reach for the landing.

Hitting a Hip or Spine

One of the most common errors in hitting a hip is that the rider travels off to the side and lands flat. The correct way is to ride to the top of the jump and then turn in the air to match the landing. This is why hips are often referred to as corner jumps. Hips can be very intimidating as the kickers have a very steep transition that throws the rider high into the air. Due to the steepness of the kicker there is often compression as the rider hits it, and this compression can suck up the speed, so often a little more speed is needed.

As you ride towards the hip you should make note of the line where the top of the landing starts. You should then aim to follow this line on your approach, as you will lose sight of the landing as you are below the take-off. With knees bent, ride on a flat base and be ready for the compression. Your time on the jump will be short, and you will experience a feeling of being rocketed into the air. As with hitting a straight jump, you will know instantly if you have made an error. The perfect area to land is high to the start of the landing, known as the 'sweet spot'. An air on a hip is a mix between a big air straight jump and a pipe air in the way that you take off on a straight jump but then have to adjust your direction to land at a different angle.

For most, a backside air on a hip or spine is the easiest side to hit (right-hand side for regular), the reason being that when you are in the air, you can easily see the landing, whereas in a frontside hip air, your back will be facing the ground and your view will be a little blind.

The biggest mistake on landing from a hip air is that the rider does not accept that they have to change direction, and tries to continue riding straight – but this is impossible and your edge would just slip out. On a backside hip air you should aim to land on your toe edge and ride at close to a 90-degree angle to the take-off. This is where the name 'corner air' comes from.

CHAPTER 14

SLOPESTYLE AND FREERIDE

Slopestyle

Slopestyle has become the most popular competitive event in snowboarding. For this reason the International Olympic Committee (IOC) has decided that men's and women's slopestyle snowboarding will be included as an event in the 2014 Sochi Winter Olympic Games. This decision recognizes the millions of young people who are already participating in the sport in snowboard parks around the world. Their aim is to add a further youthful appeal to the line-up of Olympic winter sports.

The reason that slopestyle is so popular is because the event is quite free and less formatted. The rider has to think more creatively, and there is more opportunity for personal expression. There is no set course layout, so each course varies, mostly due to factors such as the slopes changing inclines or direction. In a standard slopestyle course you would

ABOVE: Ben Kilner enters the slopestyle event at The Nescafé Champs, Leysin, Switzerland. (© Nick Atkins)

LEFT: Tonton Holland at The Nescafé Champs, Leysin, Switzerland. (© Nick Atkins)

expect to find a variety of rails and jumps, but occasionally the courses can contain elements of many of the different disciplines, so it would not be uncommon for a slopestyle rider to need solid halfpipe skills, too.

For a good score a slopestyle run is mostly judged on flow, smoothness and overall impression, and the runs are planned out in advance so that the tricks fit together with no effort. For example, if a rider lands a trick backwards, then they would be expected to ride into the next obstacle backwards (switch), because a revert or a spin to change direction to forwards could be seen as a move that breaks the flow of the run. Things like this are taken into consideration when planning a high-scoring run.

When building the best run, an athlete would need to display as many talents as possible, so each move on each obstacle should be different, and their score will be docked if a trick is repeated or is similar to another. The athlete would need to spin in every direction, as well as change the board grabs. A well mixed run with style would prove the rider's control and consistency.

With so much emphasis placed upon the flow of a run, simple, clean runs can often score higher than a more technical run with small mistakes. The common mistakes in a technical run include hand drags, reverts in direction, and lack of edge control.

Freeride

Freeriding is often considered to be the most natural form of snowboarding, in which the rider descends a mountain by riding over technical and physically challenging terrain. This terrain could consist of some steep faces with hardly any room to turn, or cliff drops that must be negotiated with little time for thought or consideration for personal safety.

Top freeriders are dropped by helicopter on the top of peaks that would not normally be reachable by most snowboarders on the piste. On the way up in the helicopter the snowboarders

Billy Morgan, Davos, Switzerland.

Top freeriders are dropped by helicopter into acres of deep, powdery terrain. (© Nick Atkins)

can analyse their chosen route for their descent, making note of obstacles such as cliff drops as well as open areas where they will be able to hit high speeds. Unfortunately the problem with this is that the obstacles look very different from the top, so it can be hard to recognize the cliff where they intended to drop off – and an error here could be fatal. Furthermore, as the descent is normally extremely steep, there is a high risk of avalanches. It is quite common whilst watching freeride events to see the snowboarders being 'chased' by a fast-flowing avalanche, and they are left with no other option than to outrun it, and hope that they can remember the correct direction for their descent.

In competitive freeriding events, the riders are taken to the peak of a mountain and are judged on the creativity with which they tackle their chosen line of descent – they are expected to take technically challenging or dangerous lines, but to make them flow with ease.

Ben Kilner , bursting through the trees at Davos, Switzerland. (© Nick Atkins)

Dan Wakeham, Boreas Pass, Breckenridge, Colorado. (© Nick Atkins)

COMPETITION AND COACHING

CHAPTER 15

PREPARATION

Once substantial progression has been reached and it is established that a solid level of experience and expertise has been achieved in the chosen discipline, a rider may begin to consider entering the competitive circuit. For freestyle disciplines they should have a substantial number of tricks within their competence that can be landed consistently and confidently. For racing and freeride, a high level of confidence is needed when riding fast with constant control.

One of the first steps in approaching the competitive snowboard circuit is to research the many different competitions that are staged worldwide, and then to target one that would be consistent with the rider's ability and experience. It would not make sense to aim too high and enter an event that is way beyond the rider's capability, as it could knock their confidence from the outset. Ideally it would be best to find smaller, local resort events to start with, and then gradually work towards a bigger event such as a national championship.

One of the biggest mistakes made by snowboarders who enter their first event

is to try to ride above their ability. A snowboarder can only snowboard as well as he or she has trained. Some competitors may feel that while riding in a competition they should push themselves to the limits of their snowboarding capability, perhaps attempting new tricks, or tricks that they have not confidently landed before. This often results in nerves and falls, as the snowboarder is not riding within their limits.

Too much nervous intensity can considerably undermine technical skill and the whole run itself. An experienced competitor will remain focused and calm, visualizing their performance with a clear idea of the course and their intended run. This may not result in the most technical or the highest scoring run, but a relaxed state of mind will be expressed in their style and control and the smoothness of their performance. Like this the rider will be rewarded with a fluid, flowing and higher scoring run.

As with the many different aspects of snowboarding, solid preparation can be the key to success in competitive

snowboarding. Careful research can enable a rider to prepare themselves and their equipment, optimizing performance. Such research prior to an event taking place should inform the rider as to what they will find on arrival at the competition site. For example, a slopestyle course could be comprised of features that the snowboarder may never have tackled before. For SBX competitions, tracks in resorts are more often smaller and safer, whilst a competition course may be significantly bigger and faster. To prepare, it may be worth practising hitting larger jumps prior to the event commencing, in order to carry out speed checks and to establish confidence.

Choosing the Right Board

Careful preparation and groundwork can assist the rider in their training and quite quickly establish any weaknesses that need to be tackled. This can also assist the rider in equipment selection, an integral part of competition preparation. Not everyone at this level of snowboarding will have the funds to spend on a wide selection of different snowboards, although it is useful to know how board selection can affect rider performance on a competition course. SBX courses can vary dramatically, ranging from fast race-style tracks to courses that are more tailored to the freestyle snowboarder and which include numerous jumps and obstacles.

For a Fast Track

If a track is fast and the obstacles unchallenging, then the race requires the

Zoe Gillings at the start gate of the boardercross, Vancouver 2010 Olympics. (Courtesy @zoegillings)

rider to cut the perfect line in the best time. In this situation the snowboarder may choose a longer board with a straight side cut, and could even consider riding with hard or very stiff race boots. Diversely, if the course includes more freestyle elements, then the board of choice could be closer to a freestyle board, so shorter in length. A shorter board would offer the rider faster and smoother movement through bumps and transitions.

For Freeride

In a freeride competition, board selection can be determined by the different types of cescents that the rider faces. For example, steep or open faces where high-speed powder riding is possible, a bigger board with a long nose would be best. For a more technical descent that may include tighter turns through rocks or trees, the board of choice may appear squashed in that it is shorter and wider – still long in the nose, but shorter in the tail. This allows it to be nimbler through challenging terrain, but it would still have adequate surface area to float on top of soft or deep snow.

For Freestyle

In freestyle disciplines such as slopestyle, the course can also vary dramatically, from a more rail-heavy competition to one that is predominantly kicker-based. If the course is more rail-dominant, then the choice of board may be shorter to enable low speed spin tricks. The edges would be less sharp so as not to catch on any rails. A course that includes a line of bigger jumps necessitates a longer, stiffer board, which will offer more stability and control at speed. The ideal board for slopestyle would be a board that works well in all conditions and situations.

Diversely, a top-level halfpipe event must conform to a competition standard size, so the choice of boards may not vary as much. In halfpipe events, the board chosen would be long enough to come up to the athlete's chin. The flex would be medium to stiff, and not too wide as the pipe rider will need to carve to hold the correct line up the pipe wall.

Preparing to Compete

If the competition is taking place in an unfamiliar resort, then it is advisable to arrive early. This would give the rider the opportunity to prepare, to assess the course, and to build a bigger mental picture regarding what to expect during the competition. It is always sensible to work out bearings on the mountain by exploring the resort, so as not to feel rushed when finding the course in an early morning start before an event. Other points to take note of are the temperature of the air so that the right type of wax can be selected. Many wax companies offer in-depth, expert information on their websites, where the snow data can be entered to provide the correct choice of waxes to mix.

While at a competition there is plenty of time for reflection as each rider waits their turn, working through start lists and heats. It is wise to take note of the layers of clothing that need to be worn so as not to get cold during these long periods of waiting. Snowboard coaches often recommend overcoats that can be put on or taken off quickly.

Building Runs

In SBX races or freeride disciplines, the objective of the run is to choose the correct line, and cut off seconds. In freestyle competitions it is to select the best scoring tricks. Big air competitions are a display of just one technical trick, so the following techniques are directed mostly towards pipe and slopestyle riders, where a well thought-out combination of tricks is required:

The first step is for the athlete to take a pen and paper and make a list of the tricks that he or she can do, across rails, pipe and kickers. Make a note of the course – for example a slopestyle course may read like this: rail > kicker > kicker > rail > wall ride. A pipe run can consist of four, five or even six hits out of the halfpipe. With this information, write out as many different run variations as possible. Place yourself in the shoes of the scoring judge, and score these runs, taking into consideration trick and grab variations, and that there are no immediate mark-down faults, such as having to change direction between tricks – that is, landing switch and having to turn round to the preferred stance before hitting the next obstacle.

By sitting down and taking the time to plan a competition run, an athlete can work out the best possible scoring run for his or her ability level. Furthermore it can inspire progression, as it will offer knowledge of what extra is needed to build the winning run.

Snowboarders waiting their turn at a competition.

CHAPTER 16

COMPETITION TRAINING

Depending on the event, there will be a difference in the training time offered by the competition hosts. For an Olympic event, training is one week, for a World Cup competition, two days, and for a small, local event it could be as little as an hour before the event starts.

Either way the training should be approached in the same manner: in good time and with careful consideration. Some snowboarders may be able to go straight into the competition mind-set and execute complicated runs with little training, but without a clear understanding of the features within the course, this could be dangerous. It is always wise to take a ride through the competition circuit and make a course inspection before training. Look at each feature individually and work out where speed is needed and where it needs to be cut down. Although the training time may be short, two to three runs should be taken without performing tricks: this should familiarize the rider with the course speed and flow.

Remember that this time is not a time to learn new tricks. Tricks should have been learnt and firmly landed out of competition training. Once the rider is familiar with the course, it should be a case of putting the tricks in place and fine-tuning them to match the obstacle.

Snowboarders can get cold while waiting their turn.

Bad weather draws O'Neil Evolution 2012, Davos, Switzerland. (© Nick Atkins)

One of the hardest things for an athlete to learn in competition is to ride to a level that is consistent with their peak performance level of snowboarding in training. There are many factors that differ between training and competition runs, which can affect physical performance and mental attitude. While training, the body's adrenalin levels will be high, the athlete's body will be warm, and the mind will be focused, and this makes riding flow naturally. However, some events may have a large number of competitors, so it can take a long time as each rider takes their turn.

When an athlete is taken out of the fast-moving, intense training environment and has to stand around for what could be as long as thirty to forty minutes, the adrenalin levels will drop, the muscles can become cold, and the mind can wander. This can also be a time when the nerves build, and at this point it may prove to be more difficult to ride with the same flow and consistency.

This ability for an athlete to switch into competition mode and ride at their best on demand is often referred to as a 'pro-switch'. Some people will be able to do this naturally – for others it may take a while to develop. With this in mind it can be a good training aid to simulate the competition format in out-of-competition training by riding intensively for thirty minutes and then taking a thirty-minute break to allow the body to cool, before dropping into a competition run.

It is also wise to train for adversity. The weather conditions in the mountain can be unpredictable and change rapidly. Before an athlete's run, it may become cloudy or start to snow. Alternatively by the time the athlete gets to take a run, parts of the course may have deteriorated quite considerably owing to the many foregoing competitors having ridden over it.

It is always a bonus if the athlete is in an early start position, because he or she will still be warm and focused. If, however, the athlete is at the end of the start list, then it is important to keep warm and in the right competitive mind set. If it is clear that there will be a long wait before the athlete's turn, then it can be beneficial to take one or two fast runs on a different slope to keep the blood pumping and the

Dan Wakeham dropping into a run at the Burton European Open 2010. (© Nick Atkins)

body warm and ready. It is advisable to do this run quickly and not to stray too far from the start gate, as the competition run could be missed.

Before dropping into a competition run, different athletes find their focus in different ways. Some have an internal focus, when they will want to be quiet and alone. External focus would find the competitor more at ease with other challenging riders, when occasionally an athlete may be found expressing their insecurities to the other athletes.

For some, nerves can drive them to complain, or to convince others that something in the course is wrong. Nerves can be infectious, so it is wise to stay clear of these people. Many competitive snowboarders choose to listen to music, which can distract the mind from unpleasant or negative thoughts. Music can fill the nervous silence before dropping in, and can often be used to provide a desired anchored response. An anchor is a trigger or stimulus that retrieves a desired emotional state. Depending on the individual, the desired response could be either calming, or the exact opposite where a song is often known as a power song. This music may provoke an explosive feeling of excitement, which can be particularly beneficial while performing in high-energy action sports such as snowboarding.

If the competition runs do not go as planned, the athlete should get up and move on, and should not over-analyse the faults. Some riders like to see instant success when they try something new, and it is important to understand that failure is not necessarily negative. Motivation and pride may be damaged, but in some situations if there is no failure, then it could suggest that the athlete is not pushing their boundaries.

CHAPTER 17

MAKING A PLAN AND SETTING GOALS

Following a competition, the experience gained by an athlete can raise their awareness of their ability compared to the other competitors. This can inspire them to contemplate their future plans as a competitive snowboarder, and what is needed in order to make the next step in a competitive snowboard career. Much like setting up a business, it is a good idea to make a clear plan. For example, the first point could be to work out the ultimate goal of the rider's intended career, such as competing in the Olympic Games.

The next step would be to research the correct avenues that need to be taken to reach that target, and then to consider other factors such as money to support travel and training, and the equipment and coaching that would be required.

Many of the above factors rely on considerable revenue to fund the developing professional. When travelling to winter resorts the costs can quickly multiply and commonly include flights, accommodation, ski pass and competition entry; in addition, funds will be needed to pay tourist resort prices for everyday essentials, which are substantially more expensive.

To help with these costs, sponsorship money is needed – but if the athlete doesn't have the money to gain the

Zoe Gillings during the boardercross, Vancouver 2010 Olympics. (Courtesy @zoegillings)

necessary competitive experience, it is difficult to reach a level that deserves sponsorship. Many young talented athletes overcome this obstacle and gain the required experience by spending the whole of a winter season in a resort. This requires only one return flight, thereby reducing otherwise exorbitant travel costs. Resort employers can often supply the athlete with a free season's pass to the mountain, and accommodation. During the time spent riding, the athlete can work to build a portfolio of photographs and video footage that can be sent to potential sponsors.

Goal Setting

Although many people set goals in everyday life, very few people set their goals effectively. However, many studies have shown the benefits of goal setting to improve performance in sport. In a survey of leading sports psychologists working with US Olympic athletes, goal setting was found to be the most used technique to aid performance. Goals must become the building blocks of success in snowboarding. The athlete can use these as a challenge, to measure his or her performance and offer a sense of achievement when the goals are met. Goal setting should become a major part of building a snowboard progression plan, and goals should be set for both short- and long-term motivation and success. Those who are not setting their goals effectively may have limited success, because the way we set goals is as important as the goal itself that we hope to achieve.

In order to set goals an athlete must first realistically establish the level of their ability: this will become the starting point. In setting a goal, athletes are committing themselves to a journey from their established starting point and on to their ultimate goal. They must question where their strong points lie, and where there is potential for growth. They may then need help from a coach to come up with a strategy that will enable them to achieve their technical goals time and time again.

Apart from technical ability, the two main areas that affect performance are fitness and mental skill. Technical ability is the ability to make intricate movements consistently and habitually. Mental skills include imagery, concentration and emotional balance.

The S.M.A.R.T. Criteria Model

S.M.A.R.T. has been used for many years as a model for effective goal setting. It is a good way to express goals so that the potential for achieving those goals is dramatically increased.

S = Specific

In order to set effective goals, they must be specific. The more specific an athlete can make the goal, the more they can increase their chance of achieving it. Setting a goal to ride better next time is not being specific. A more specific goal would be to land the new trick correctly with a certain desired grab, or to hit the podium within the next three events.

M = Measurable

For a goal to be effective an athlete must be able to measure whether or not the goal has been achieved. Hitting the podium will be a clear sign that the goal has been reached, but landing the new trick just once out of several attempts with poor style or control would indicate that the trick has not been truly learned and is not ready for competition.

A = Achievable

The goals set need to be within the realms of possibility. If a goal is set too far out of reach, the athlete may start with the best of intentions but get disheartened and not commit to completion. It could be wise to plan more short-term, achievable goals, and establish a time frame that allows that final goal to become a reality.

R = Realistic

This is not a synonym for 'easy', but more a case of 'do-able'. A realistic goal may cause the athlete to push to reach their skill level, but would not be so far beyond their technical ability that they would risk injury.

T = Time-bound

It is difficult to achieve a goal without setting some kind of time constraint, and for this to be really effective, the time set should be as specific as possible. It could be a case where an athlete might say: 'One day I want to win the X-Games.' Without specifying a time frame, five years can pass and the same person might be saying exactly the same thing, so that chasing that goal becomes much like running a race without a finish line.

CHAPTER 18

SPONSORSHIP, NATIONAL TEAMS AND CAREER MANAGEMENT

Many snowboarders are under a completely false apprehension as to what it is to be a sponsored rider. Some believe that by reaching a high enough level in their chosen sport they simply deserve to be paid. However, the reality is that for lifestyle-driven sports such as snowboarding, the sponsored athlete enjoys a much more developed and mature role, playing a key part of a brands marketing plan.

Advertising campaigns can use a large percentage of a brands marketing budget. For example, to run a double-page advert in a magazine that is produced in high numbers and has a global distribution can cost thousands. Many brands prefer to give equipment to athletes who appear

regularly in editorial features, be it in magazines, on video or in online blogs. The pictures or clips that display clear branding ensure that these brands maintain an important presence in the media. It is not unusual to associate a top athlete with a brand. Many aspiring riders respect accomplished snowboarders, and if a brand is associated with that athlete, it can gain considerable credibility within the target demographic.

The average age of a professional snowboarder is decreasing, and understanding the mechanics of marketing and how to behave professionally and to appreciate how the media functions is a considerable requirement for a very young rider. Without a knowledgeable parent or manager to negotiate contracts, the young athlete can be overlooked.

Sponsors expect their athletes not only to excel at snowboarding, but to be social media experts and web designers, connecting with the target audience and networking with the media and with film producers, photographers and editors. Upholding strict brand values and practices, and professionally projecting the brand's required image, are an intrinsic part of the sponsored athlete's commitment. A 'marketable' snowboarder is a profitable investment for a brand. For younger or less extrovert athletes it may be harder to achieve, but it is a part of the job that should not be overlooked, as it is often required from a rider when they are forging a successful career.

Joining a National Team

Joining a national snowboard team can

An advertisement with Danny Kass for Grenade.

require a seasonal core cost to cover coaching and administration, but there are often many benefits which make it worthwhile for an aspiring athlete. For example, by travelling with a larger number of people the overall cost of travel can be greatly reduced; furthermore team vans can carry athletes and their equipment between resorts, so there is no need for flights, public transport or hire cars. Also, accommodation deals for having larger group numbers can be sourced, and pass deals are often offered to national teams to encourage them to train in their resorts.

One of the biggest advantages is to be able to build camaraderie with the other top athletes. The knowledge and

Dan Wakeham in an advertisement for Head snowboards

experiences gathered can be passed between team athletes as they learn to progress together, and this can improve the quality of an athlete's riding standard immensely.

The Coach's Role

A coach's role is not simply to be the critique of an athlete's ability or potential. Rather, he or she is a team leader, in charge of organizing travel and bookings. The snowboard coach oversees all training and competition runs performed by each athlete. A video camera will be used to film the training and events, and the footage used for detailed video analyses; moreover many coaches take photographs of each athlete in action.

The athletes will then use the photographs and footage to promote themselves and their sponsors online. An informed athlete will add humour to each video edit to create a viral effect when it is posted around social networking pages, appealing to the youth market that largely constitutes the snowboard demographic. Sponsors are then able to re-post the videos or use the photographs in their advertising campaigns. This will add to the brand's credibility, which will then add to the value of the athlete to the brand.

A modern snowboarder will be business minded. Many own laptops and smartphones so they can maintain an online presence. Cameras are a necessity to keep blogs updated with fresh content and video reportage.

Coaches are often more experienced, and can offer sage advice not only regarding snowboard progression, but also on snowboard career management.

Career Management

If a talented athlete is under the age of eighteen, then a coach may act as the responsible adult, allowing the youth to travel freely between countries and be looked after at events. The athlete must understand that if he or she chooses to become a professional snowboarder, then

their main focus must be their constant improvement at snowboarding. This requires discipline, and for many young, talented riders their ambitions in snowboarding can become unclear. But if an athlete isn't performing, then the sponsors will fall away. The coach is the

boss, and if he or she feels that the athlete is under-achieving due to partying or misbehaving, then that athlete will be discarded from the team and they would not be able to take part in national or Olympic qualifying events.

Once a snowboarder has worked hard

Jamie Anderson takes home US $15,000 for first place at the Burton European Open 2011. (© Nick Atkins)

and reached a high level, and has started hitting podiums, he or she can take big money in a short time-frame. Competitions will regularly pay out €10,000 for a win, and prize money is paid all the way down to tenth position.

There are sponsors who not only pay an athlete's salary, but will then pay a prize match incentive bonus payment. Furthermore the brands have to protect their investment, so successful competitive snowboarders can expect good travel comforts and accommodation. From the athlete's point of view, if that is the target and they feel they have what it takes, then there are many routes they can take to get started. The first step would be to secure initial financial support.

As a national team member an athlete can be eligible for funding, and there are many different avenues that can be explored. Talented athlete scholarship schemes can be sourced through governing bodies; however, many of these are only available as long as the athlete remains in some kind of education, and they are frequently offered free courses. The type of courses often chosen by a rider are ones that will benefit them both in their current snowboarding career and for their life after snowboarding. The following are courses that are commonly chosen:

- **Media** courses that offer training in Photoshop or video editing programs as well as blogging techniques. Others can offer the skills needed to be in front of a camera, such as TV presenting.
- **Marketing** courses that offer the skills to promote a product: essentially the career-minded athlete may become the marketable product.
- **Athletes** can become trend setters on the slopes, so a course in fashion may help them have input into brand design, or even start their own brands.
- **Photography** courses will offer the skills needed so that the athlete can capture their experiences as they travel the world, and record some breath-taking scenery.

Winners of the BEO 2011 men's slopestyle.

- **English or literature** courses could help improve the athlete's ability to write creatively; their literary efforts could then be used in magazines or on blogs.

For a young athlete it may be hard to think beyond their dream of becoming a professional snowboarder, but as they progress as a professional in their chosen sport, the experiences they gain in their career may replicate many that you would expect in starting any new business; these might be:

- Money and time management
- Negotiating contracts
- Building and working to a brief
- Setting targets

All these skills can help to build a strong CV, making the athlete stand out in the eyes of future employers.

CHAPTER 19

FITNESS AND INJURY

Physical fitness training is an essential part of progressing in any sport. The physical preparation required in action or extreme sports can differ slightly from that needed in, for example, cycling. By keeping to a strict training and diet plan an athlete will inevitably get fitter and stronger, and will be able to cycle faster and for longer. One cannot assume the same will happen with a snowboarder's technical progression. While participating in action sports there is always a risk of serious injury or death. This requires a certain mental preparation and ability to be able to overcome the fear and relax in dangerous situations. This is something that most will develop with experience as they learn to be confident in their ability to execute a manoeuvre in a safe and controlled manner. For some, this ability may come more quickly than it does for others.

In the early years, snowboarding, skateboarding and the lifestyle that surrounded the sports were considered to be anti-establishment or against the mainstream, as explained in an earlier chapter. Although snowboarding has developed hugely and essentially has matured into an accepted mainstream sport, there still seems to be a divide between anti-establishment snowboarders and modern, progressive, competitive athletes. This is not necessarily a negative, as the variation keeps the sport exciting and less uniform than other Olympic sports.

This could lead an athlete to consider that spending time in the gym is not socially acceptable, and it is often the case that young athletes can get disheartened after training hard for a competition to then be beaten by someone who is less fit.

However, there are many advantages for a snowboarder to be physically fit, such as:

- The physical ability to be able to train/ ride harder and for longer
- To be able to withstand flat or heavy landings that may have normally resulted in a crash or fall
- Injury prevention and quicker recovery times
- Having the physical strength to withstand the compression received while riding up large jumps or hips

The general or common somatotypes of the top snowboard athletes vary between snowboard disciplines. Freestyle riders are often slightly shorter, and are lean with toned muscles; this is an advantage for the gymnastic-like movements that are performed while executing tricks. Racers are often bigger and more heavily set, as this added weight is an advantage while trying to gain speed to cut seconds in their race to the finish line.

Although these may be the ideal or most common body shapes for each discipline, this is not to say that an athlete must conform to one of these stereotypes to be the best. In snowboard cross, some tracks may favour the smaller rider as he or she can be more nimble and turn on a tighter radius. Likewise in freestyle, a shorter rider may have the advantage of being able to perform tricks more easily, with less speed, whereas the bigger or heavier rider will be able to pick up speed or gain momentum more quickly, especially after a mistake.

Snowboarding requires a good level of cardiovascular preparation and a need for explosive fitness. This will enable the athlete to ride for long periods of time and produce fast, powerful movements such as tricks or aggressive turns. With most freestyle or action sports the progressive rider must expect to take a few hard, unexpected crashes, and even

some badly judged landings would take a toll on the unfit rider.

A general fitness programme for snowboarding would put an emphasis on building strong legs and good core strength and flexibility. The training plan should cover a good level of overall fitness, though it could be considered a disadvantage to build big muscles on the arms and shoulders – adding this extra weight to the upper body would raise the athlete's centre of gravity, which could compromise the rider's stability. Any good personal trainer would be able to study the needs for each individual athlete and tailor a gym plan that would be specific to the athlete to aid them in their chosen discipline.

Not every athlete will have the opportunity to work with a personal trainer or have regular access to the gym. A creative athlete will find there are many things that can be done at home or in the great outdoors that will raise the level of fitness, such as running or cycling. Many parks or walking trails will have pull-up bars or picnic benches that can be utilized. Lunges, squats, sit-ups and press-ups can be done anywhere, and require no costs or equipment. Gym balls are inexpensive to purchase, are great for building more stability, and can be easily packed into a bag and taken on the road.

There are numerous suspension training devices (aka bodyweight training) on the market that are also ideal for the travelling snowboarder. These kits seem to be extremely popular at gyms and sports clubs across the world, owing to their simplicity and versatility. The kits can be used almost anywhere, and can be mounted to a wall or to a doorframe. Every part of the body's muscles are catered for, not only targeting the key muscles that regular gym equipment will

Single leg squats.

work on, but also smaller supporting muscle groups, which again adds to greater core stability and overall strength.

Fitness Plan

Some examples of exercises that can benefit the progressive snowboarder are given below. The movements can be done anywhere as long as there is sufficient space to move, and require no special equipment; the workout should be repeated on a regular basis. During each workout, the exercise movements should be repeated in sets or reps, the number of reps entirely depending on the individual's level of fitness.

Start off with a cardiovascular warm-up such as a brisk walk that leads into a light jog. This will bring up the muscle temperature and lead to a higher breathing rate.

Single Leg Squats

This is a great test of both leg strength and balance. Stand on one leg and lift the other by bending the knee. Allow the body to drop down in a slow and controlled movement. The lifted knee can be straightened in front of the body to help with balance and lateral stability. Remember to keep good posture with the chest high and the foot flat on the floor at all times. Once the knee is fully bent, push up and straighten the leg to finish the movement. This move can be made much easier by using one of the before mentioned suspension training devices.

Side Plank

Lying on one side, lift the body up so that is supported by one forearm and the feet. Hold this position for one minute, and then repeat for a minute on the other side of the body. This is a simple but effective exercise that can benefit the spinning and flipping movements performed while snowboarding by strengthening the oblique muscles.

The plank.

The Plank

Lying face down, lift the body so that the forearms and toes support it. Keep the torso straight and rigid, and the body in a straight line from head to toes, with no sagging or bending. This is a great abdominal exercise.

Walking Lunges

With the hands behind the head and the chest high, drive the knee into a full stride. Control the landing and sink into the leg, allowing the knee of the rear leg to drop towards the floor. Stand on the forward leg with the assistance of the rear leg and lunge forwards to repeat with the opposite leg. Aim to start with five to ten lunges on each leg.

Side plank.

Walking lunges.

Mountain climbers.

Mountain Climbers

Place the hands on the floor in a press-up position. Bring one leg up and bend it under the body with the other extended. While holding the upper body in place, alternate the leg positions by pushing the hips up while immediately extending the forward leg back and pulling the rear leg forwards under the body, landing on both forefeet simultaneously.

Plank to Knee Crunches

Start in the plank position and hold it for ten seconds. Then with the bum high and a strong back, bring a knee up and into the chest in a slow and controlled movement. Straighten the leg again, and back into the plank position. Repeat by bringing the other leg into the chest.

Pre-Competition Warm-Up

Competitions often start early in the morning to maximize the short daylight hours in the winter months, so those snowboarders who consider they are not good 'morning people' have a disadvantage from the offset. The warm-up starts from the moment the alarm goes off in the morning. No one can expect to get out of bed, get dressed and then drop in and explode into their best performance. It is not only the muscles that need to be warmed up, but the brain needs to wake up. Many snowboarders feel that they ride better in the afternoons, and this is mostly owing to having enough time for the whole body to be warmed through and for the aches and pains of the previous training day to be shaken off. With this in mind, if the athlete knows in advance that the event will be starting early, then it makes sense for him to prepare his body clock by

getting up early for at least several days before the event itself. This would result in less of a body shock when getting up early in the morning to compete on the event day itself.

The morning pre-competition warm-up should be light and slow so as not to cause premature muscle fatigue. The chances are that the body will already be tired from previous training days. A brisk walk followed by some light dynamic stretches would constitute a gentle and effective early morning warm-up. This could include arm swings, trunk rotations, inward and outward hip rotations, high leg kicks, kickbacks and knee swings: these are gentle, slow types of stretching through the joints' range of motion. Some of them will be similar to the kind of movements that will happen naturally in freestyle snowboarding. It should be enough to bring up the muscle temperature, to get the blood pumping and the body limber but not to the point of tiredness.

If it is possible to make some fast snowboard runs before arriving at the event, this will raise the adrenalin levels, which can help to override any pre-competition nerves and keep the athlete's focus clear. As the time draws nearer to first dropping in for a competition run, the athlete should increase the intensity of the warm-up by jumping or jogging on the spot. Once again this will raise the breathing rate and muscle temperature so that the body is ready to perform at its best.

Plank to knee crunches.

Daily stretching.

Snowboarding uses explosive bursts of energy that often require energy production faster than the body can adequately deliver oxygen to the muscles. In these cases the muscles generate energy anaerobically. This energy comes from breaking down glucose into a substance called pyruvate. When the body has plenty of oxygen, the pyruvate is broken down aerobically, but when the muscles are starved of oxygen, as they are with the explosive movements in snowboarding, the body converts the pyruvate into a substance called lactate. A side effect of the high lactate levels that accumulate in the muscles is acidity left in the muscle cells. If the body is allowed to slow down gradually and the oxygen becomes available again, the lactate reverts back to pyruvate.

It is very important that an athlete should cool down after intense snowboarding sessions so that the lactic acid can be pumped clear of the muscles to avoid achy or heavy legs when waking up on the following morning.

Cool-Down

As the name suggests, the cool-down needs to have the opposite effect on the body than is expected from the warm-up: the muscles need to be cooled, and the heart rate reduced to its resting rate. Start with a five-minute jog that slows into a brisk walk: the body will decrease in temperature and remove the waste products (lactic acid) from the working muscles.

Find an open space and start with some static stretches. Whereas the dynamic stretches in the warm-up consist of controlled leg and arm swings that help the body limber up, static stretches are more appropriate to the cool-down as they help muscles to relax, realign muscle fibres, and re-establish their normal range of movement. These stretches involve gradually easing into the stretch position and holding the position, such as touching the toes.

Daily Stretching

Many people may question whether there is a point to regular stretching or maybe they don't see enough benefits to take the time to do it. Some may regard stretching as just a warm-up, and something that you do before or after the more high intensity exercise occurs or begins. All athletes, regardless of their sport, will require a basic level of general all-round flexibility. Some of the benefits include the following:

Injury prevention: Good flexibility is the body's automatic defence mechanism to overextension of the muscles. When a snowboarder crashes or tumbles, the body can be thrown into difficult or uncomfortable positions that could result in injuries.

Reduced muscle tension: Stretching realigns muscle fibres, which speeds up the recovery process after a hard workout. When fibres are intertwined, scar tissue requires more time to heal.

Reduced risk of low back pain: This is a common ache for snowboarders who spend a lot of time standing sideways and squatting over their legs. Flexibility in the hamstrings, hip flexors, quadriceps, and other muscles attaching to the pelvis, reduces stress to the low back.

Relaxation and reduced stress: There may be many stresses in training or competition as the athletes push themselves to reach goals or targets. Stretching with slow and deep breathing is an excellent way to fight that tension and calm the body and mind. Within minutes after stretching, everyone feels better. There is something inherently healing and pleasurable about stretching.

Injury

Fear is an incredibly strong emotion, and when people experience a dangerous situation the body sounds the alarm and triggers increased production of adrenalin. Adrenalin speeds up the heart rate, increases energy supplies and raises the blood pressure. This is a great feeling, and is why many are attracted to the speed and excitement that comes with snowboarding. Unfortunately, once in a while a bad calculation or human error occurs and some snowboarders don't get away with the risk they have taken. Broken bones and head injuries are not an uncommon sight for the mountain ski patrol when helicoptering injured people away to hospitals. This is why many resorts try to encourage the use of helmets in their terrain parks.

The athlete who remains within the limits of their ability can avoid many injuries. This is not to say that progressive riders should not fall, as falling is a part of learning, but observing and considering carefully the potential dangers before dropping in can help to avoid dangerous situations. More often than not it is the less experienced snowboarders who sustain serious damage to themselves. The experienced snowboarders may be tackling bigger jumps and challenges and flying further, but by learning how to prepare to fall, most of the time a heavy impact can be minimized by dropping to the ground, sliding, and keeping the arms in and away from danger.

Some of the injuries commonly sustained by advanced snowboarders are bruised heels or ankles, damaged knees or ligaments, dislocated shoulders, broken collar bones, wrist hyperextension sprains and whiplash of the neck. Most of these are easily resolved with time or minor surgery, and the athlete can be back training in as short a time as six weeks, although some injuries may remain untreated.

If, however, an injury is left untreated or not allowed to heal properly, then it will persist as a niggling pain that can affect an athlete's focus and motivation – it will be constantly on their mind while training or competing, and could lead to other injures or crashes. This is because the mind can subconsciously compensate for things such as incorrect weight distribution between the legs when landing so as to protect the injury.

Recovery

The most challenging element of recovery is allowing enough time for the body to heal. Many snowboarders will have a high tolerance for pain, which is why the rider can get back up after a crash without being too scared or shocked to try again. This tolerance may mean that the injured athlete is persuaded to return to training before the injury has had sufficient time to heal. A sports physiotherapist will be able to analyse the injury and draw up a recovery plan.

Achieving Joint Stability

After an injury it is essential that the joints are allowed to return to correct alignment. A good rehabilitation programme will include exercises that target joint stability. Once an injury is on the mend there are many simple exercises that will help to improve mobility as well as build strength and restore the full range of motion to the injured area.

The first step for achieving joint stability after an injury would be to assess the joints for misalignment or structural defects. A physician or therapist will check the joint alignment and test for weakness or defects in the soft tissues (tendons, ligaments, and cartilage): correcting these may require taping or bracing, or possibly surgery.

Once the joints are returned to proper alignment, joint stability is addressed and specific exercises are prescribed to help restore function. These exercises target balance, proprioception, range of motion, flexibility, strength and endurance. In order to make a full recovery from an injury an athlete must participate fully in their rehab programme.

Visiting a physiotherapist regularly can become costly, but a disciplined athlete should listen to the advice given to them so they can repair their bodies in the comfort of their own home or gym. For example, if the damaged area is an ankle, the sooner the sprain is treated, the sooner the injury will recover. By getting immediate attention, the ankle can be better in a matter of days. If nothing is done and the athlete chooses to ignore the pain, then he or she could potentially end up with a sprain that can take weeks or months to heal properly. Most of the damage from a sprain comes from the associated swelling, so the main goal is to reduce this swelling as much as possible – and to do that, every second counts. One of the most popular acronyms to remember if you get a sports injury is PRICE, which stands for Protection, Rest, Ice, Compression and Elevation. Using these immediate first aid measures is believed to relieve pain, limit swelling and protect the injured soft tissue.

A General Rehabilitation Programme

After an injury, a general rehabilitation programme would include a range of motion exercises and a gradual progression to full weight bearing. One simple exercise is to draw the letters of the alphabet with the toes, from which there should be a gradual progression to weight-bearing exercises.

Thera bands are lengths of rubber that come with different levels of resistance. The band can be looped around a solid object such as a table leg, then with the heel of the foot kept in a solid position and the band high on the foot (around the toe area), simply move the ankle in sideways movements to make the band stretch and release; move the ankle around and gently try to target its different muscles. These are known as proprioception exercises, and can be performed not only as recovery but also as part of an injury prevention programme.

In addition to our eyes and inner ears, there are special receptors in our joints (proprioceptors) that provide information about our position in space. For example, balancing on one leg will reinforce and strengthen the receptors in the ankle.

The following exercises can be used to rehabilitate, strengthen and build good body balance. Add the exercises slowly over several weeks, according to how they are tolerated by the body:

- One-leg balance: try to stand on one leg for 10–30sec.
- Do the same exercise with the eyes closed.
- Balance board ball toss: while balancing on a wobble board (which you will find in most gyms), catch and toss a small medicine ball with a partner. Alternatively at home balancing on a pillow has a similar effect.
- While balancing on a wobble board or pillow, perform ten slow, controlled half-squats.
- Single leg spot jumps: hop from spot to spot on the floor.

CHAPTER 20

CROSS-OVER SPORTS

During the 'off snow' months (in summer time) many snowboarders choose to partake in other sporting activities: not only will these help to maintain their fitness level, but many demand the same attributes and skills as in snowboarding. The chosen sports are often other board sports such as surfing and skateboarding, which require many of the same balance and turning skills. This doesn't mean that because someone is good at one sport they will naturally be good at the other, but it may be that in learning to adapt to similar board control techniques in each sport, progression in the others may be accelerated.

There are different turning techniques in snowboarding depending on the snow conditions, but the riding technique for firm snow may be closely matched to skateboarding. The weight is generally distributed closely between both legs and the turns are initiated by leaning the board from side to side; this allows the skateboard trucks to turn, or the weight to be pushed into the side cut of the snowboard, encouraging the board to roll into a carve turn.

In deep powder snow, on the other hand, riding a snowboard may be more closely likened to surfing. Here, the bodyweight is pushed to the rear leg and the turn is initiated through the back foot, just as it would be as the surfer pivots the board over the surfboard's fins.

Lucas Brammall, nose grind.
(© Nick Atkins)

Surfer Nick Atkins does a backside slash.

For people who are transferring their skill from other board sports it may feel natural to be standing sideways on a snowboard while in motion, although it may be intimidating, difficult or less natural to newcomers. Similarly, people who may be coming to snowboarding from a skiing background would already be able to read the mountain terrain and snow conditions, and they may also have a good understanding of how to use the snowboard edges effectively for controlling the travel of direction, the speed and, most importantly, the ability to stop.

Downhill Mountain Biking

Athletes can go downhill mountain biking in many of the resorts that are used in the winter months for snowboarding. Most resorts open several chair lifts and cable cars to take the walkers and bike riders up to the peaks. Not only is it great to visit the mountains in the summer months, but it can be a great experience to use the mountain in a different way. For those who are familiar with the resort's winter pistes or trails, it is useful to see the resort without snow, especially for freeriders, as it can help them to build up an understanding of the terrain and the rocks or dangers that may lie beneath the winter snow.

Snowboarder Gregor Samuels, a keen cross-over sport enthusiast at Les Deux Alpes, France. (© Nick Atkins)

Another skill that can be gained from riding a bike down a mountain at speed and which is similar to those skills found in snowboard cross and freeriding, is the ability to evaluate the terrain quickly and gauge potential hazards. In both sports the rider will need to read the ground that lies ahead, and quickly take note of details such as the condition of the ground or the tightness of a gap between trees, and then adjust their speed or riding intensity accordingly to prevent a fall or injury.

Indoor Freestyle Snowboarding

Freestyle snowboarding has become very gymnastic. The flips, spins and body movements in the air require a high level of spatial awareness, and it is now common to find indoor freestyle training facilities in the resorts that have the best snow parks. These facilities have jumps that are covered in dry-slope matting, an artificial, plastic, snow-like alternative. These jumps have foam pit landings, so the snowboarder can experiment with new tricks, flips or rotations with less risk of injury than if they were to attempt the same trick on a real snow jump.

Trampolining

Trampolines are commonly used to experiment with new body movements and to gain spatial awareness. Being able to repeat the movements again and again with each bounce, the athletes can build muscle memory and develop control and stability in the air.

Jamie Nicholls trains in Woodward at Copper, which offers one of the most unique training facilities in the world.

Nick Atkins on the trampolines in Woodward at Copper training facility, Copper mountain, Colorado.

Diver Tom Daley. (© Penny Cross)

Diving

When training on a trampoline the amount of airtime could be a lot less than it would be in the course of a snowboard jump, meaning that the tricks might have to be rushed. Diving can offer a more similar experience to that of riding a snowboard jump, because the process of running in a forward direction along the board when attempting tricks means that they would flow in the same way as they would if moving forwards on a snowboard. The increased airtime would mean that a flip or spinning movement would have to be well timed. The rotation speed would need to be controlled either by pulling the arms and legs in tight to speed the flip, or by opening out the body to slow the rotation.

Parkour

Many gymnastic clubs will open their facilities to alternative sports such as 'parkour', otherwise known as free running. This is where participants use or move around obstacles in a way that wasn't initially intended by the architect. An example would be a skateboarder sliding down a handrail instead of walking down some steps. A parkour enthusiast might scale their way down the outside ledge by jumping, vaulting, rolling, running or climbing, and using the environment in a creative way. There are many similarities in this to a snowboarder arriving at a new snowboard park or freeride descent. He or she is faced with a selection of obstacles or terrain, and must choose a creative, alternative and different line while adding a selection of technical moves that are better than those of their competitors. This kind of creative thinking is useful in that a snowboarder will then tend to stand out from the crowd, and catch the eye of judges, photographers or sponsors.

CHAPTER 21

QUALIFICATION FOR COACHING

While snowboard training, many athletes will naturally coach each other as they bounce knowledge between themselves to gain a greater understanding of what is needed to build a smoother, more technical or higher scoring run. Some riders may find that they have a natural ability to lead and offer tips and knowledge, whereas others feel the need to be told or inspired. It can come to a point where the leaders feel that they are better at explaining the tricks than they are at executing them, and this might encourage them to take an interest in coaching, and in gaining the relevant qualifications.

There is a considerable difference between a snowboard instructor and a coach, although both terms are used interchangeably to imply the transference of snowboard knowledge between one person (teacher or coach) to another (a student or athlete). Before any person can think about hitting a jump, racing to the finish line or taking on a near-vertical descent down a mountain face, he or she will need to be taught the basics of snowboard technique. This is teaching or instructing, and it is a one-way process where the instructor's information or

Dan Wakeham talks through the tricks with an athlete before he sets off.

knowledge from past experience is offered to the student.

With coaching the process is much more two-way. The coach imparts the knowledge, the athlete questions to clarify, and may also add comments based on their past experience, therefore transferring some of their knowledge back to the coach. The coach may then adapt their original comments based on the athlete's contribution. The athlete then attempts the trick or move, and both are able to provide feedback based on the athlete's feeling and the coach's observation of the move itself. Instantly the learning process has become much more two-way.

As an instructor leads a lesson, he or she must demonstrate the basic movements with a correct technique so that the pupil can observe and attempt to replicate it. It is essential for a coach to be able to snowboard to a high level, and often the coach has been an ex-professional or an expert in some other similar field. The coach is expected to understand the moves, motions or biomechanics needed in action, but is not expected to demonstrate the move or trick himself. It is all relative to the ability of the group or individual. For example, at a lower level of coaching it may be appropriate for the coach to offer a demonstration, but at a world-class level, if he were able to demonstrate a double cork 1080, then possibly he should have entered the competition himself.

Each individual athlete will respond differently to certain coaching techniques, and it can take time for both the athlete and the coach to build a bond or an understanding of how each other works. Often it can be something that happens very quickly, or in some cases not at all,

which can be factored to the athlete's receptiveness or openness to the coach's input. There are many dangers that come with progressing in snowboarding, mostly due to the coach's need to push an athlete to the edge of their ability or comfort zone. The athlete must then trust both the coach's judgment and advice.

The athlete will quickly sense if the coach is truly sure of the advice he or she is giving, and if trust is lost then it will be hard to regain. With this in mind, if the coach is unsure about any advice then it is wise to try to work out the problem together with the athlete. Some inexperienced coaches may feel that they need to have an answer for all situations, but they must remember that coaching is a two-way process. The athlete may feel that they can talk to a coach in a way that they couldn't talk to one of their peers or teammates, as the coach must remain neutral and non-biased.

Group coaching is often run in a set session administered by the coach. During this session, communication between the individuals and the coach may be little to none. The coach is there to watch, film and oversee the session, monitoring each athlete while making mental notes on each individual, as well as the good and bad points of the session. The coach may pull an athlete to the side if they feel there is something that needs to be corrected. Drills may be set for individuals who are having problems with a movement, where the drill is explained to increase the athlete's mental visualization of it, and its execution to enhance the feeling and muscle memory for the movement. The athlete will then be asked for feedback, to remember and relate how it felt. Once the coach is satisfied that the athlete has grasped the concept and practice of the

drill, they may be asked to go back to the movement they were having problems with. This and other drills should be practised and applied until the trick or move is considered robust or consistent enough to be executed in competition.

Qualification

Qualification also differs between an instructor and a coach. The focus of instructor training is on the teaching of snowboarding from a completely novice standard to pre-competition. The areas covered include the physics of snowboarding as a form of controlled motion down a slope, starting with learning how to explain in depth the dynamics and basic essentials such as the sideslip and turns.

The coaching course focuses on a more advanced level of snowboarding, be it SBX, freeride or freestyle. The coach has to create training programmes that will match the individual athletes or group. These performance plans are mostly based on target setting. The coach will work with each athlete to gauge their individual ability so that a personal performance pathway can be created.

In summary, the differences between teaching and coaching occur mainly in the depth of knowledge that is exchanged, and the focus of that transfer. There are also differences between the level of qualification and the focus of those qualifications between teaching and coaching. However, the main similarities lie in the fact that teaching and coaching are both essentially athlete centred, and excellent communication and planning skills are needed for both.

OPPOSITE: *Professional snowboarder Dan Wakeham coaches Aimee Fuller. (© Nick Atkins)*

END NOTE

Snowboarding has enjoyed a fast-paced progression from its formative years when it was widely unaccepted in mountain resorts. Snowboarders were typically refused access to the slopes, and the few courageous riders who dared to attempt admission were habitually cast aside. Now, snowboarders are encouraged to visit resorts to train in and out of season.

The resorts themselves spend millions constructing and maintaining the best terrain parks and freestyle training facilities. Snowboarders are internationally accepted athletes, endorsing huge corporate brands through marketing and brand promotion. The industry surrounding snowboarding and action sports has also developed in the form of new snowboard brands and innovative product development, allowing the sport to radically advance.

International ski bodies have always typically governed snowboarding, but as snowboarding has matured, the knowledge of the sport and how it should be run has enabled snowboarders to govern snowboarding themselves. Many have started brands, created magazines and documented the sport in its most beautiful mountainous environment through epic photography or cinematography. Technology has enabled people to push boundaries with their equipment and instantly spread their experiences to the world via the internet.

For those young riders who have a talent for snowboarding, a career in snow sports can become a realistic option. By joining a competitive team, the rider can enjoy international travel to global competitive events, and be inspired for a future career in life after snowboarding.

Snowboard trips or holidays can also be a great way to make friends for either the experienced professional or the recreational boarder. Ski resorts are full of active, healthy people, and are ideal for those who like to burn energy and follow an activity on their holiday.

School leavers who are looking for a 'year out' often head out to spend a season in the mountains, honing their snowboard skills. To find out more please consult the Useful Resource section below.

Snowboard trips or holidays can be a great way to make friends, for either the experienced professional or the recreational boarder.

USEFUL RESOURCES

British Ski and Snowboard: http://www.teambss.org.uk/

The British Snowboard Association (BSA): http://www.snowboardclub.co.uk/bsa

One Snowboarding: http://www.onesnowboarding.co.uk/

INDEX

Other Sports Titles from Crowood

BMX RACING
TOM JEFFRIES
WITH IAN THEWLIS

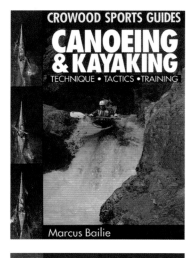

CROWOOD SPORTS GUIDES
CANOEING & KAYAKING
TECHNIQUE • TACTICS • TRAINING
Marcus Bailie

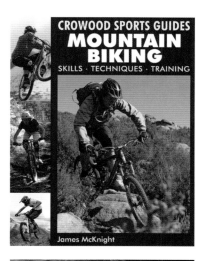

CROWOOD SPORTS GUIDES
MOUNTAIN BIKING
SKILLS · TECHNIQUES · TRAINING
James McKnight

Off-Road Running
Sarah Rowell

CROWOOD SPORTS GUIDES
ORIENTEERING
SKILLS · TECHNIQUES · TRAINING
Carol McNeill

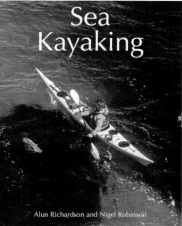

Sea Kayaking
Alun Richardson and Nigel Robinson

CROWOOD SPORTS GUIDES
SKIING
TECHNIQUE • TACTICS • TRAINING
Fred Foxon

TOTAL FITNESS
*An Advanced Training Guide
for the Sportsperson*
Nita A. Martin

Trail and Mountain Running
Sarah Rowell and Wendy Dodds